THE PATTON BROTHERS

LAUGHING ALL OUR LIVES

Brian and Jimmy Patton

with Matthew Coniam

2

Introduction 5

Early Days 8

Stepping Into Show Business 18

Pattons on Parade 26

Ladies and Gentlemen – The Patton Brothers! 35

The Boys at Butlins 44

The Boys on the Box 54

Doing the Rounds 62

Good Companions 75

Playing the Palladium & Working with Ronnie 94

The Show Must Go On 107

Pantomania 117

Still Going Strong 137

4

INTRODUCTION

"You're always learning in this business, and it's great to watch other pros at work."

That was something Frankland Grey, boss of 'Britain's Dead End Kids', said to Jimmy when he joined the act back in 1946, and he was certainly right.

We've been a double act since 1954. We've had our arguments, naturally, but blood is thicker than water and being brothers we've always been great pals. We've worked everywhere in our career, all over the world, from the smallest working men's clubs to the most famous variety theatre in the world: the London Palladium. At the height of our career we'd do a pantomime every year, along with a summer season, and then in the spring and autumn we'd play the clubs. It's been a great life with some wonderful memories. If we told you everything, this book would probably be ten times as long! Choosing what to include and what to leave out has not been easy.

But there were some memories that we just had to share. Like the wonderfully happy season we spent in *Aladdin* at the Churchill Theatre, Bromley, in 1995/96. All the cast were lovely people. We'd never met any of them before, but we all got on like a house on fire. Gloria Hunniford was top of the bill, and she was delightful: from the first minute she seemed like an old friend. Bonnie Langford was Aladdin and she was lovely to work with too.

But the one who really kept everything bubbling along was Christopher Biggins. He played Widow Twankey and he was just as charismatic offstage as on. On the last day of the run Christopher arranged and presented a comedy awards ceremony on stage in between shows. The cast, crew and front of house staff all sat in the audience as he and Gloria announced awards for campest performance of the season, most over the top portrayal, biggest ham, and many more!

We were all in hysterics, and just when we thought it was all over, Christopher said: "We can't finish without mentioning two lads who have been in show business all their lives. This year is their fortieth consecutive pantomime together without ever missing a performance. Ladies and Gentlemen, the Patton Brothers."

He and Gloria presented us each with a lovely statuette, each engraved with our names, and underneath: '40 Years Pantomime Celebrated at the Churchill Theatre Bromley 1995/96'. With that, the whole company stood up and applauded. It was a lovely moment, and one we'll never forget.

In this book you'll find many more happy memories from our long career in the business. We hope you'll enjoy strolling down memory lane with us as we remember our experiences in the great days of variety, summer seasons, holiday camps, TV and, of course, panto. We'll also tell you about many of the stars we met along the way. We worked with big stars, small stars, stars from Britain and all over the world, stars of stage and screen, stars on their way up (and sometimes down), and, of course, all those great unknowns with talent and enthusiasm for whom the breaks never came. As Frankland Grey predicted, it's been great to watch them all, and we never stopped learning.

We have toured all over the country and eaten up many miles. We are the longest serving double comedy act in the country having done over 60 pantomimes including the summer ones. The career that we have enjoyed has been wonderful, and we'd do it all over again at the drop of a hat. It's been a wonderful life, and we've loved every minute of it.

EARLY DAYS

Jimmy:

I wouldn't have changed my childhood for anything. There was no television back then, so radio was the thing. I still remember listening to my favourite shows: *Music Hall, Happydrome, Take It From Here* and *The Billy Cotton Band Show.* Wonderful memories. And of course, going to the pictures was a real treat. At the Premier Cinema or the Tivoli near our house in Kimberworth, Rotherham, I used to thrill to Errol Flynn, Tyrone Power, Lana Turner and Rita Hayworth. The seats were four pence or nine pence in old money – that's about two pence or four pence nowadays. If the picture had an A certificate you had to be accompanied by an adult, so we just used to go up to any man that came along, give him our money and say, "Will you take me in please, mister?" You couldn't do that today! It was an innocent world then.

I used to write to all the Hollywood stars, and I've got hundreds of autographed photos that they sent me. I'd wait for the postman to arrive every morning, and what a thrill it was when a letter arrived postmarked Burbank, California. I used to wonder if I'd ever meet any stars in my lifetime, and I've been very lucky that in my career I've worked with and met hundreds of wonderful stars and friends.

It all started on August 20th 1931, when I was born in Bromley, in Kent. Mum and Dad were touring the country in a revue show. Mum was a dancer in the Rodney Hudson Girls, and Dad was a comedian who worked under the name Gene Patton, well known on the music halls, in variety, revue, pantomime and radio. As well as a comedian he was a soft shoe dancer and siffleur. Well done if you know what a siffleur is without having to look it up! For the rest of you – it's a professional whistler.

During World War II he was principal comic in the RAF Gang Show which toured India and Burma (he was a Flight Sergeant small arms instructor). His feed in the show was a nineteen year old drummer and impressionist who did rather well for himself in Civvy Street – Peter Sellers. Just before he died, Dad gave me a bill of that show and it has pride of place on the wall of my study. Peter's mother was very well off and she wrote to Dad and said that after the war she wanted to put on a show starring Dad and Peter. Dad often told me about the plans that he and Peter used to discuss. Everything was arranged, but unfortunately Dad was demobbed a couple of years before Peter, and as he had a young family to keep he had to go off in a touring revue, *Spivs and Drones*, with Ernie Lottinga. Nothing ever came of their plans and he never met Peter again.

I was the oldest of six children. After me came Brian, Sheila, Colin, Barry and Paul. We all followed mam and dad into show business except for Colin. He became a mechanic, and a very good one. He always fixed our cars for us when they went wrong. He's retired now and I often go to the match with him when I'm at home – we're fervent supporters of Rotherham United. We lost our beautiful sister Sheila to that dreadful cancer. She was a lovely girl, and was a dancer in our younger days. The other four Elliott boys are still going strong, I'm pleased to say, though you might know Paul and Barry better as the Chuckle Brothers!

When I arrived on that summer's day in 1931, Dad was over in Eire doing a concert party summer show in an open air theatre at Bray Head. Later in life he told me that on opening night a couple of hard men appeared back stage and said to Dad: "What music are you playing at the end of the show?" Quick as a flash he replied 'Phil the Fluter's Ball'. That made them happy and off they went. In those days, of course, back in England the closing music was always 'God Save the King' – not so appropriate in Southern Ireland!

There were always rows in our house when we were kids and election time came round. Dad was a staunch Labour supporter and mum was Conservative. All us kids followed mum's opinions, and I've been a Tory all my life. I was only young, but I remember how disgusted I was with the British people when they voted in Attlee's Labour government after the war, and let down Winston Churchill so badly after all he'd done to get us through with his bulldog spirit.

Dad's real name was James Patton Elliott. He came from a family of miners in Hetton-le-Hole, County Durham. When he left school he worked down the pit for one day and decided it wasn't for him. So he ran away and joined an act touring the variety theatres, Walter Ford's Boys. Mum was born Amy Frances Harman. She did shows with dance troupes in Holland and Germany before meeting Dad in a show in England. Her sisters Elsie and Ethel were dancers too. So it just seemed natural to me that I'd follow in their footsteps. Apparently my first appearance was at the age of two, on stage at the Pavilion Gourock in Scotland with Mum and the girl dancers, dressed as a little soldier and doing a song and dance.

Whenever Dad came home and opened his case you sensed the 'smell of the greasepaint'. I remember going backstage with him when he was doing pantomime at the Empire, Rotherham, and the Grand Theatre, Doncaster. He usually played Buttons in *Cinderella.* I clearly remember walking past the dressing room of the Ugly Sisters and saw them in their frocks, talking very strangely for a young lad! Then a girl playing principal boy... All very weird and wonderful!

During World War II Brian and I did charity shows in Wickersley Village Hall for Lord Beaverbrook's Speed the Tanks fund. We did sketches, scenes and comedy routines, and the packed audiences loved it. I was only small then, and we used a very tall, lanky stooge so it was very funny. Donald Shearing was his name. Our mums did the costumes, and we had proper programmes printed. We even got a personal letter of thanks from Lord Beaverbrook.

I left Maltby Grammar School at the age of fourteen. I liked it there: I enjoyed English, Art and Music, and I was good at football and cricket too. Mr Rush, the headmaster, told me that I ought to stay on and take my school certificate, but my heart was set on following in Dad's footsteps and making a career in show business. For a while I did a double act with my dad in the working men's clubs. We'd do shows on a Sunday lunchtime, and as we walked in the smell of smoke and stale beer really made me feel sick. I vowed that I'd never ever smoke or drink alcohol, and believe it or not I've stuck rigidly to that all my life.

Brian:

I was born on December 13th 1933. Mum had had Jimmy and carried on touring, but after I came along she needed to give up dancing, so we settled in the centre of the country in Rotherham, South Yorkshire. This is because it was on the LMS and LNER railway lines, and Dad couldn't drive and never had a car.

Both Jimmy and I were born at Grandma's house in Bromley. We never knew our maternal grandfather, who died before I was born. He was a photographer named Herbert Palfrey Harman, which is where I got my middle name. He died in his dark room, and they had to force the door open as he had died behind it.

I nearly didn't make it to my first birthday, thanks to whooping cough. We were living in Maltby and had outside toilets. It was a nice day and Mum needed to spend a penny, so she asked Dad to keep an eye on me, and if I coughed, to pick me up quickly and pat or rub my back. She had only gone for a moment and I must have done a quick cough. Dad missed it, or thought I'd stopped, but when she came back she had a slightly blue baby in the pram, my face turning all sorts of colours. She screamed and picked me up, and the neighbours came running, some even saying "Oh, he's gone, love, give him to me", but she wouldn't. A man came running down from up the road, took me off Mum and pumped my little chest. He did mouth to mouth resuscitation and eventually my heart started again. I was put into cold and hot baths and got through it. They said that I might end up with a weak heart, but here I am in my eighties, still working. Magic!

We moved a lot over our younger years, always in and around Rotherham. Bramley, Masborough, Wickersley, Maltby — you name it, we've been there! Jimmy and I and our sister Sheila were in Wickersley when war broke out. Jim and I used to go up into the front bedroom, upstairs, and cheer and whoop when flashes went off over the sky in Sheffield. It was like fireworks to us. The Germans only ever dropped a couple of bombs over Rotherham, in the park. Sheffield had the steel works, making planes, tanks and bombs, so they and Coventry got the main punishment. We were told that the bombs that were dropped on Rotherham were the ones that were jettisoned as the aircraft left for home. We saw the Doodle Bugs too! You would hear the drone, and when it stopped the bomb would come down and you'd wait for the explosion. We had a shelter in our garden in Wickersley, and we loved it when the siren went off. It was all just great excitement for us kids. I still remember the smell of the paraffin that was used for lighting the heater and lamps. In fact, we felt let down when no siren went off, as we had beds in there!

I remember travelling to school on a trackless 'bus' with an electric cable to the overhead. (You may remember it as a trolley bus.) I did well at school, and ended up as third top of my class. But like Jimmy I had the show business bug. I used to have dancing lessons at Miss Thompson's school of dance, at the top of Ship Hill in Rotherham. I loved it.

Jimmy:

It was Sunday September 22nd, 1946. I was only fifteen, and I'd never been away from home before. I was setting off to join a variety act called 'Britain's Dead End Kids'. Earlier that year I had won a talent competition at the Regent Theatre in Rotherham. The first half of the show was a variety bill and the second half was Tony Gerard's 'Search For a Star'. I did a few gags, and a comedy song and dance to 'Down Where the Daffodils Grow'. Dad was in the first half, and when I told him I was entering the talent contest he said, "Don't tell them you're my son!" He was afraid I'd show him up! I was thrilled when I won but not half as thrilled as Dad was. "That's my lad!" could be heard all round the theatre! The first prize was £18 and as a treat I went to see England play India in the test match at Old Trafford.

A few weeks later there was an advert in the *Rotherham Advertiser* saying: BOY WANTED TO JOIN VARIETY ACT. There was a bus strike at the time, so Mum and I walked the two miles into town so I could audition. Frankland Grey, the boss of Britain's Dead End Kids, was there with the lads. There was Peter Kenyon, who was the oldest and a brilliant xylophonist. Gwynfryn Arvon Thomas – we called him Taffy – had a lovely baritone voice that was always a big hit with the girls. Derek Hamer was a very good comedian, and a very nice, quiet lad. Ronnie Dukes was a terrific tap dancer with a great personality, and a bit of a tearaway. Eric Bluff had a beautiful soprano voice, and Teddy Alexander, who I palled up with, was a real jack of all trades: comedy, magic, and the ukulele. Then there was me! They must have liked me because I joined the act immediately, opening September 23rd at the Accrington Hippodrome in Lancashire.

I wasn't very big at fifteen so I called myself 'Wee Jimmy Elliott – Little but Good'. Well, I had a *huge* suitcase, and when Mum saw me off at Rotherham rail station that morning I was staggering along the platform! Ronnie Dukes, who was later to become a big star, was seventeen and quite a well-made lad, so he carried my case for me. On that Monday evening I got out my little make-up box and was just about to put on my Leichner's 5 and 9 greasepaint when Ronnie said, "Hasn't the boss told you?" "No," I replied. "We're the Dead End Kids, and he thinks it would be more realistic if there was a little coloured boy in the act." With that, he handed me a stick of black greasepaint and I smeared it all over my face. Of course, when the boss came in he went mad. Out came the liquid paraffin and it came off – eventually! Many years later I recalled that experience when Eammon Andrews surprised Ronnie Dukes on *This Is Your Life*. But that first night on stage was everything I'd ever imagined it would be. The footlights, the orchestra pit, the other pros in the show, the audience reaction... a wonderful experience!

The headliner at the Accrington Hippodrome was ventriloquist Peter Brough, with his doll Archie Andrews. There were some excellent variety acts, too, with something to please everyone. There was Cire the

Command Performer, a marvellous illusionist who filled the stage with flags. (No one was allowed on the side of the stage when he was on.) Then there was Koringa, the Only Woman Fakir in the World. She did an act with crocodiles and snakes. And Donna Delbert, lady fire eater, who was later arrested when it was discovered that *she* was a *he* – and a deserter from the US army!

STEPPING INTO SHOW BUSINESS

Jimmy:

The boss of the Dead End Kids, Frankland Grey, was in his early seventies and had been a performer all his life. He was excellent as the Dame in pantomime. He was always giving us advice, and I clearly remember him telling us to go to the Odeon to see the young comedian in a film called *Mr Big.* That was the brilliant entertainer Donald O'Connor – he was only about twenty then, and he went on to a marvellous career. In 1947 when I was 16 and playing at the Grand Theatre in Clapham I went to the Theatre Royal, Drury Lane, to see the big new American musical *Oklahoma.* The young leading man was called Harold Keel. Later, of course, he became the legendary Howard Keel. I think Howard has a better ring to it than Harold, somehow. One of the best shows I've ever seen was at the London Coliseum in 1947: *Annie Get Your Gun,* starring a wonderful singer and actress, Dolores Gray. She was brilliant! Each time we came to London I'd dash up to the Coliseum to see a matinee. It was Lew Stone and his Orchestra in the pit, and what a thrill it was when the overture started, playing all those fabulous show tunes. The big number was of course 'There's No Business like Show Business'. How true that is!

Sometimes we'd work with a big star when they were just starting out. It was in 1947 that I first met Roy Castle. We played the Hippodrome,

Lowestoft, and the following week we weren't fixed anywhere, so we had a week's stop over there. That week *Happiness Ahead* was at the Hippodrome and Roy was one of the star performers along with Fred Brand. Roy had star quality even then, and he did a great song and dance routine to 'Alexander's Ragtime Band'. We all became friends and the cast of our show played a charity football match against their company. Years later Brian and I did *The Good Old Days* on BBC TV when Roy was starring. It was great to see him again, and he got us to go on with him at the end of his act and do an impromptu eccentric dance routine.

In 1946 we played the Shakespeare Theatre, Liverpool, and there was a comedy music act on the bill who did a very funny act. No patter, just visual gags, and they all played instruments. They were called the Bill Hall Trio, and the trumpeter went on to a very successful career on his own. That was Spike Milligan. The same year we did a week at the Hippodrome, Chesterfield. On the bill was a young comic called Bill Waddington, who told gags and sang comedy songs while playing the ukulele. We didn't meet again until 1982 when Brian and me appeared with him in *Mother Goose* at the Empire, Liverpool. It was during that season that Bill told us that he'd been offered six weeks' work in *Coronation Street* – and he ended up playing Percy Sugden for the next fifteen years! Then he came to Brian's wedding, met our sister Sheila, and ended up as our brother in law! That's show business! Sadly, Bill passed away in 2000.

In these early years we had train call every Sunday, when we all travelled from town to town. All the touring revues travelled by train, and we'd walk up and down the corridors to meet the pros from the other companies. The girl dancers always looked fabulous! It's funny, but whatever show you were in, you always thought the girls in the other shows were better. (As the old saying goes: the grass is always greener...) One particular Sunday I'll never forget. As the train pulled into Crewe station, I was dashing along the platform looking for our reserved compartment, when there sitting in the corner of the carriage was Sir Cedric Hardwicke. For me, a young newcomer, it was a great thrill to see someone of his calibre. I'd seen him in all those Hollywood films, and it hardly seemed possible that here he was in person. Another time I saw Arthur Lucan, who I loved to see as Old Mother Riley at the movies.

The scene for the Dead End Kids' act was a sort of 'back street' cloth, with a lamppost and a dustbin, and we'd come on fighting and making a noise. The boss would come on dressed as a policeman and say, "Come on, lads! Do something worthwhile – if you've got any talent, put on your own music hall!" Then one of the lads would go forward as compere and we'd all do a little act in turn. My comedy song was called 'I'm Not All There'. We were all dressed as ragamuffins until the finale, when Ronnie Dukes came on as a sailor and did 'The Fleet's In'. Then we all came on in white American sailor's uniforms and finished up dancing to 'Anchors Aweigh'. We had a new boy join the act later on called Bobby Wildman, from Golborne in Lancashire. He was a whistler and did bird impressions. He was a nice lad and he did a good act, whistling to the lovely old song 'In a Monastery Garden'. What we didn't appreciate was being woken at 2 o'clock in the morning to chirping sounds, and Bobby saying: "How's this for a blackbird?"

All the lads got on very well, and we had some great fun. Every Sunday when we arrived in a new town we used to get settled into our digs and then find out where the theatre was. We'd look for the posters to see what our billing was, and what times the shows were. It really was an exciting life, meeting new acts on the bill each week, and making new friends. We used to be able to 'pass in' to all the pictures on complimentary tickets, so we saw good films. The older lads used to play snooker and I longed for the day when I'd be eighteen and allowed to play in the billiard halls.

The lads taught me how to play cards and our favourite game was solo. We used to play on the train every Sunday, and in the dressing room too. We played for money, but not big stakes. It's a great game and we really got carried away. One night we were playing the Gateshead Empire. Top of the bill was Sam Browne who was very popular on the radio. We were following a funny comedian called Hal Blue. He was billed as 'Hal Blue – Cleaner than Persil'. He got good laughs all week, but this Friday night they were really noisy up in 'the Gods'. He only did a few minutes of his act and nobody was listening, so he walked off. They shouted through the tannoy: "Dead End Kids – you're on!" The cards and money flew everywhere as we belted down the stairs and dashed on stage just as our entrance music was playing. We did okay, as we were a boisterous act and had a big finish.

One night Eric Bluff was singing 'The Holy City' in his lovely soprano voice. The rest of the lads sat around on various parts of the stage listening. Well, the lad who was sat on the dustbin must have had too many beans for dinner, because he suddenly let rip with the loudest jam tart you've ever heard. It echoed from the dustbin and boomed right around the theatre. The audience fell about and so did the lads, apart from one. He was so embarrassed he went as red as a beetroot. No one dared sit on that dustbin again!

Brian:

My first job in show business was also with the Dead End Kids, at the Theatre Royal, Loughborough. This was in 1949, so Jimmy had been with them for years by then. It was the last week they were performing, and I was to do a routine to 'The Fleet's In', the spot that Ronnie Dukes (among others) had previously done in the act. My dancing teacher taught me two choruses but when I did the band call, for some reason I finished my routine after one chorus! I was mortified, and was in tears in the dressing room, but the boss, and Jimmy and the lads, said, "Do the same routine again to the second chorus". I did this the whole week, but the toilet was used nightly before we went on! The act finished that week, but hopefully not because of me!

At this time my Dad was touring in variety, and Billy West was on the bill with his Harmony Boys. Dad mentioned to Billy that I was a good singer/dancer/comedian and Billy immediately said he'd take me on! Mum came over with me to Halifax Palace by bus, and I joined Billy and the boys, and Billy's daughter, Enid Margaret. We performed numbers like 'The Lady in Red' and 'Jerusalem'. That wasn't my only contribution to the bill. In my first week with them, I also helped out brother and sister act Vic and Jo Crastonian - they asked me to yank a bear rug off stage when Vic fired a gun!

There had been a mining disaster and we did a charity concert at Swansea Grand Theatre. It was compered by Richard Attenborough and featured a young Harry Secombe performing his renowned comedy shaving act. This famously got him sacked by a boss at Bolton who said, "You're not shaving on my time!" Sam Costa was also on the bill, as well as Ken Morris performing his piano stuff. I received a photo from Harry and Sam Costa which I still have today. We also did a week's variety up in Edinburgh and I passed in to see the brilliant Bela Lugosi in *Dracula*, playing the main part live on stage, as he had done in the film. I still remember the excitement as he appeared on the stage in a cloud of smoke. Another week we performed at Chiswick Empire Theatre, and top of the bill was the film star Bonar Colleano. I got his autograph, and in his room was a young film starlet, Susan Shaw, who had made films like *Dance Hall*. Don't worry - they later married!

Jimmy:

I played the Empire, Belfast, with the lads in 1947. We'd been at the Tivoli, New Brighton, the previous week and we travelled over by boat from Liverpool. That was okay, but coming back there was a raging storm in the Irish Sea. We all thought it was great fun at first watching the waves roar up higher than the ship, and being tossed about like a cork. But as it went on we all ended up staggering back to our cabins one by one, and I've never felt so ill in my life. The boat was packed, and several of us lads were sharing a cabin with two professional wrestlers, Jack Pye and his brother Harry. The boat was rolling like mad, and I was in the top bunk. I was as sick as a dog over the side, and my pal Teddy Alexander who was underneath copped the lot. I remember Jack Pye saying, "Oh, you've started me off now, kid!" and vomiting into the sink. It was the worst storm they'd had in years, and the crew were all suffering too. There was sick all over the cabin floors and the deck of the ship. I've hated traveling by sea ever since.

When I started working for Frankland Grey I was on thirty shillings a week, and I used to send ten shillings of that home to Mum! But the boss did pay for our digs and traveling expenses. He cut corners when he could, though. After the Accrington Hippodrome our next venue was the Hippodrome in Bury. As it wasn't far, he hired a lorry, and all the lads travelled in the back of this open lorry – with all the scenery. Luckily the weather was fine! Some of the digs were dodgy to say the least, but we took it all in our stride.

In the digs in Bury there was a big bear rug on the floor, and being lads we used to hide under it. After a couple of days we all came out in a rash and couldn't stop scratching. The doctor told us we'd all caught scabies, and we had to daub this lotion all over ourselves! It would normally be full board so you couldn't choose what food you wanted. There was usually an open fire, so as soon as the landlady left the room I used to throw the fat from the meat on to it. Sometimes she would come back in and wonder why the fire was spluttering and hissing.

When we had to cater for ourselves in digs there would be six of us, and the boys were given ten shillings each for the week. So when it was my turn I'd have the £3 and get the food to last the seven days. Mince was a popular favourite, and sausages. We all survived somehow!

PATTONS ON PARADE

Jimmy:

I often wonder how my life might have turned out if different things had happened. For example, in 1947 I was sent for an interview to Elstree Studios. I had no idea what for. I was very shy back then, and hardly had a word to say for myself. I was full of confidence on stage, but very different off. I was later told by Frankland Grey that it was to see if I might be right for the part of Oliver Twist in the famous David Lean film! C'est la vie!

In 1948 when I was touring in a show called *Youth and Laughter.* Frankland Gray was still the boss, but it was presented by Wickham Productions and Eddie Jones. I was principal comedian in the show, and I got £4 a week, plus accommodation and traveling expenses. It was at this point that I changed my stage name from Jimmy Elliott to Jimmy Patton. My dad's real name was James Patton Elliott and he had started off in show business as Jimmy Elliott. However there were lots of Elliotts about in the business at that time, so he changed it to Gene Patton.

Brian:

My first pantomime was in 1949/50. It was at Dudley Hippodrome for 12 weeks. Top of the bill was Duggie Wakefield as Widow Twankey and Reg Varney as Wishee Washee. The speciality acts were Wilson, Keppel and

Betty and 'The Two Pirates'. The Pirates were great: Jock would lift his partner, a little fella, on a wire and say things like "One finger!" Or he'd start to do the splits and say, "Half tonight, half tomorrow night". If there were no laughs he'd say, "Is the curtain up?" Great pro lines! To close the first half, I played a dragon's head - sometimes half the dragon would go one way, and half the other! It was packed out all season, twice a day. I used to stand outside the Hippodrome upstairs on a steel staircase watching hundreds of double decker buses coming in every day. Jimmy was in the RAF at the time, and came over and saw the show before he went with the forces to Ceylon, now Sri Lanka.

Jimmy:

I stayed with Britain's Dead End Kids until 1949 when I did a summer season at the Happy Valley, Llandudno, in a concert party called *The Concord Follies,* presented by Charles Wade. It was an open air show and done in a beautiful setting. Dad was principal comic and I was second comic, so I used to feed him in double acts and sketches. On a lovely day there was nothing better, but if it rained the show would be cancelled. When the weather was overcast I would pray for rain so I could dash down to the pictures or go to the Arcadia Theatre to see *Catlins Showtime.* I went to the Pier Pavilion one night and Vic Oliver was topping the bill. He was brilliant and I admired his slick patter and infectious humour. Also on the bill was a cute little girl singer with pigtails who sang 'At the End of the Day'. She was only twelve or thirteen, but she had a beautiful voice. It was a young Julie Andrews.

It was at the end of that summer season that I was called up to do my National Service in the RAF. I did my square-bashing at Bridgeworth in Shropshire and I was in 10 flight. The NCO in charge of us was Sergeant 'Jankers' Jordan. He was firm but fair, although we were all scared of him. I didn't mind all the bull, as I'm a tidy person anyway, so my boots were always shining, as were my buttons. They did a concert at the camp so I volunteered and did my comedy, song and dance act and the lads loved it. The Sergeant was so impressed that I got a 36 hour pass to go home. (It can't be bad!)

After that I did a driving course for six weeks at Weeton, near Blackpool: three weeks on Hillman cars and three weeks on three ton lorries. When I'd passed out as an MT driver I volunteered to go overseas for the rest of my eighteen months service. I spent three weeks sailing on the Empire Trooper from Southampton to Colombo in Ceylon. I was sea sick at first, but gradually got used to it.

Again they asked for entertainers to put on a show and I was the first in line and produced the show and rehearsed the other volunteers. We gave six performances on various nights, on a makeshift stage built on the deck. That was fine apart from one night in the Bay of Biscay, when it was very rough. The ship was rolling and the piano was doing the same. We managed somehow, but it wasn't easy to tap dance with the ship rocking from side to side.

Ceylon was fabulous, though. A wonderful climate, right up in the eighties and nineties. Stunning scenery, too. I thoroughly enjoyed my time there, even though my eighteen months National Service was extended to two years because of the Korean War. I arrived in Ceylon on April 5th 1950 and left in October 1951.

I played cricket for the MT section and played football for the RAF at representative matches against the Ceylon Navy and Air Force. I was good at centre forward and my record was excellent. In 49 games over there I scored 49 goals. But I also damaged the cartilage in my right knee, and I've had trouble with it ever since. The surgeon gave me Pentothal and snapped my knee back into position. Then I had it in a splint for three weeks. It's never stopped me doing all the tap dancing I've done all my life, but there are certain steps I know I mustn't do or the cartilage will snap out of position again. It happened again just a few days before we were due to *The Vera Lynn Show* for the BBC. They couldn't snap it back at the hospital until they put me out with Pentothal. The nurse told me afterwards that as the doctor twisted my knee it was like the sound of a rifle shot as it went back into position. My leg was heavily strapped as I did the show, but nobody ever knew! As I've got older, if it happens now I can manage to snap the cartilage back myself. I should have had an operation years ago, but never got round to it.

My two best pals were Geoff Key and Tich Manley. We were together right from our training days. We got paid once a month in the RAF, and the money never seemed to spin out. But Tich always seemed to have money somehow, and we used to borrow from him on the last week of every month. Before sailing to Ceylon everyone was supposed to have several injections for various diseases, but Geoff and I refused and said that we didn't believe in them. So that was that! But at the end of our National Service more inoculations were due and we were told that if we refused them our demob may be delayed. So we had the lot! Two or three in each arm – it was agony driving those lorries for a couple of days!

We sailed back and were demobbed at Lytham-St-Anne's, near Blackpool – freezing cold after that wonderful climate in Ceylon! I wouldn't have missed my National Service for anything, and I think young people today ought to be conscripted too. Everyone needs to be taught discipline and respect for others and for yourself.

Coming out of the forces, I was keen to pick up my show business career where I'd left off. Luckily, Frankland Grey fixed me up as guest artist in his show at the Queens Park Hippodrome, Manchester. I bought myself a stage suit, straw hat and tap shoes, and off I went. As well as doing my own act I did a double act with a pretty blonde girl, Gena Mae. From there I went into pantomime, playing Billy Crusoe in *Robinson Crusoe* at the Empire Theatre, Tonypandy, in South Wales. It was great for me playing principal comic, and I made a success of it. That was followed by a tour in a strip show, *Temptations.* Television was coming in, so to fill the theatres they tried using strippers. The audience was mainly men, but they enjoyed the comedy too!

Brian was now doing *his* National Service in the RAF, but we had reached a decision. When he was demobbed in 1953, we would start working together as The Patton Brothers.

Brian:

In 1950 I was still with Billy West and his Harmony Boys. We did a broadcast on radio which was supposed to be with Frank Randle topping the bill, but he had been out fishing on his boat in Morecambe Bay with Gus Aubrey (his feed in the show) and hadn't appeared at the rehearsals. The radio broadcast used another comic, Albert Burden, to do a spot ("I'm happy when I'm hiking"). Meanwhile Frank was unhappily ranting and swearing at the hotel staff who had tried to waken him in time for the broadcast. Frank did eventually appear in the afternoon looking very classy, not like his image on stage or screen (ragged and false teeth removed).

We did a spot and a singer, Mel Dix, performed a solo. He was exceedingly nervous, and forgot the words, and Billy walked forward quickly to the microphone and shoved the words in front of Mel! Mel did then perform the song fluently, although one could hear the pause when the programme was broadcast!

We did another radio broadcast in London called *Up and Coming*, which was a talent show, aired weekly for new acts. We won it that week. Then the pantomime for 1950 was *Aladdin* at Wimbledon, with Clarkson Rose (of *Twinkle* fame) and comic Eddie Reindeer. Summer season for 1951 was at Glasgow Pavilion, with top Scottish comic Tommy Morgan (known as 'Clairty, Clairty'). Jack Milroy came in for a fortnight with his wife. They did a spot where he was a popstar and she came up from the audience as a fan shouting "We're all coming tonight!" (It sounds rude, but got big laughs!) Jack was great, and Jimmy and I worked with him some years later, a lovely guy and great comic. Jack was the only Scottish comic we got to work with who didn't seem to worry that we were also comics. Some of the Scottish comics would use Jimmy as a straight man and me in more of a comedy role!

When we were in variety at the Windsor Theatre, Bearwood I saw a bill for my favourite film star, Donald O'Connor. The great Donald! Jimmy and I loved watching him in films. I knew he had been doing the London Palladium, but the bill said Birmingham Hippodrome, so I phoned the theatre. The manager said, "If you come down, you can go in and see him." As we closed the first half of the show, my pal Ken and I got a bus into Brum, and ran up the aisle. It was great to see Donald in the flesh. We stood at the back and watched him in awe. He mentioned that the next song he was to sing was 'Be My Love', and said, "This is a song by a new big star coming up – Mario Lanza." He finished his act doing a great tap routine and running up the wall doing a flip over, as he did in *Singin' in the Rain*, which wasn't out yet! Brilliant!

I auditioned at Attercliffe Palace, Sheffield, for Mildred Crossley, who had *Happiness Ahead* on tour, with Roy Castle in it. Mildred asked me to go over to Elland near Halifax to learn a few routines, which I did, in case I took over from Roy while he did his National Service. She offered me the chance but I didn't do it, because I too had to do my National Service a few months later, and I was enjoying being with Billy West and the boys.

Pantomime in 1951/2 was at the Swansea Empire – now no more. Max Wall was top of the bill. I even did a tap routine with Max, and he had tap shoes made out of slats of wood from America. (Roy Castle told us later that he too had owned a pair!) We did marching at first in tempo, whilst Max performed the steps – a great routine. Max also finished his spot playing the guitar and singing. He was appearing each weekend on the radio in *Variety Bandbox*, travelling up to London to do it from Swansea. The King died during the pantomime, so we had a day off in respect for his passing.

After that I had to do my National Service. I went to Padgate on the train, and we were picked up from the station and taken to the camp to be kitted out in our RAF uniform. The black boots had to be really shining. The bubbles had to be burnt off with a poker and then we had to shine them. We were then sent 'square bashing' and I was sent to RAF Weeton, near Blackpool. Eight weeks of hell! I wanted to do the same as Jimmy and tried to sign up to be an MT driver (he couldn't drive when he signed up, but managed to be taught there and then). As for me, I could only sign up to do the same if I signed on for seven years. Forget that! I wrote down suggestions like telephonist and PT instructor, but eventually got my fifth choice of cook! I went to RAF Innsworth in Gloucester for an eight week course, and at the end I had to provide a seven course meal. I did well, except that I singed the bottom of the apple pie. But luckily they didn't try a piece of it, and it looked good, so I passed easily. I was then sent out to a camp. I was sent to Middleton St. George, near Darlington, where Dad was at the Hippodrome with top Geordie comic Bobby Thompson ("the little waster"). I went out with one of the girls in the show, but nothing came of it.

I got sent out to Croft Airport, cooking for night flying because our camp were the aerobatic champs. One pilot said, "Elliott, I'm going to take you up in a plane and dive at the ground!" I said "Oh no you're not!" (It never happened!) I had a good two years out there, and then when I came out in 1954 Jimmy and I got together for a magic career of over 60 years and still counting.

LADIES AND GENTLEMEN - THE PATTON BROTHERS!

Jimmy:

We bought red suits, red tap shoes and red bow ties. We did our first show at the Greaseborough Social Club in Rotherham. Everything went well, so we went over to the famous City of Varieties theatre in Leeds and did an audition for Bob Grey (the Ace Showman). He thought we had what it takes, and he got Philip Hindin to sign us up for two years with the Mannie Jay Agency.

My brother and I started our act in March 1954 at the Empire Theatre, Woolwich, in a touring strip show called *Honky Tonk.* We toured the British Isles for 18 months at a different theatre each week – great experience for a new act, as you can imagine. We were the comics in the show, doing all the sketches and scenes as well as our own act. There were four strippers in the show: Tess, Dora, Alma and Pauline. Three of them just showed their boobs, and got ten shillings a week extra. Alma went that little bit further and got one pound a week extra! They were smashing girls, though, and just did it for the extra money.

We used to tear 'em up with our act at the end of the show, in which we combined knockabout comedy and fast, hectic tap dancing. Again, it was great training. Ten minutes was as long as you got to make an impression in a variety show, but in cabaret they wanted at least half an hour or forty minutes. So we had to work out lots more routines and cross patter, establishing the style and rhythm of the act that did us proud from then on.

Brian:

Jimmy and I auditioned at the City Varieties, Leeds for Bob Grey and Philip Hindin. They loved our act and we signed immediately to Phil and they took us on a week or so later. In *Honky Tonk* we took over from the musical act Noble and Denester (one of whom, Del Denester, became manager at the Windmill in London).

We took over at Salford Hippodrome and the lead comic was George E. Beck. He'd had an operation on his stomach after mistakenly swallowing something that had to be removed. He was a good comic but he wasn't well, and after about a month Jimmy and I took over as the principal comics while Bob Grey mainly did his act. He would do impressions of people and did one saying, "My impression of Jules Bledsoe who sang 'Old Man River' in films before Paul Robeson!" We thought, "Who?"

We went on at Woolwich Empire and there were girls in the box whooping at Jimmy and me. I did a dance with prostitute-type girls leaning on a lamppost! The girls in the box really whooped! We did great for laughs doing one sketch where Jimmy came on as a young boy with a catapult, talking to his Mum (Billie Roche). She told him to "go and pick up her winnings at Slippery Sam's place!" The tabs opened to a small table with three of us sat around it playing cards. Jimmy came in with the catapult and we told him to sit down and join the game. We were playing poker and all said what drink we wanted. Jimmy, as the young lad, said "I'll have a Coke and a clothes brush!" He'd drink the Coke, leap in the air, then fall flat on his back rolling around, get up, pick up the clothes brush and brush himself down, and sit down. A funny gag!

We toured with this for 18 months all over the country. There were two girl dancers in the show Alma and Tess. Alma stripped off completely, and was told not to move at all. Billie Roche came backstage and said "Alma, keep your eyes still, it looks like you're counting the house to see how many are in!"

We did our first summer season at Rhyl Amphitheatre for Mrs. Billie Manders in the *Quaintesques*. The top comic that summer was Jay Martell. Our pianist was Jay Barrie who did a double act with Jimmy Duncan. There were two guys also doing comedy – Al Dixon and Al Rogers. Al Rogers stayed in the area for most of his life, and even came to see us in *Chucklevision* in Llandudno. Al Dixon later became 'Old Walter' who sat at the bar in *Emmerdale Farm* for five years and never said a word. He was driven by taxi for every episode!

We were asked back the following year but they wanted Jimmy as the comedian, and us to do our act. I found out that Jimmy was getting more money than me, and I did say at the time that if that happened again, then the act was finished! Jimmy understood and we never argued over money again! We were invited back for two more years on the same money as each other, which was great. We had different people in the show each summer. One year we had ventriloquist Ray Alan. Issy Bonn was his agent, and he took Jimmy and I onto his books but never really did a lot for us. Ray asked us if we'd write out one of our acts for him and the doll to use, which we thought was rather cheeky! He said he'd be working different places and night clubs than us!

The following summer season we were at New Brighton as second comics to an Irish comedian, Charlie Ellis, who performed his comedy similar to Max Miller with a blue and red book of jokes. He was a very funny guy and it was a very enjoyable season. The show was for Jackson Earl whose lady friend was Peggy. We had a lovely double act from Scotland Lloyd and Vi Day in the show, and Peggy took a fancy to Lloyd and the boss didn't like it. Lloyd had had an operation to remove a mole on his chest and it grew again and he had to have another operation. Jackson Earl made him play piano and sing that night! Sweat was running down his face! Unfortunately, Lloyd only lived until Christmas time. He was a lovely lad, and a sad loss to the business.

There had been a murder in Rotherham during that season and two CID men came all the way down from Rotherham to take our fingerprints and they were testing everyone in the area, even though we hadn't been there at the time! They were nice enough guys, but brought out some rude photographs which they thought we may like to look at! (We didn't bother!) We never heard from them again, and we still don't know what happened!

The next summer was at Llandudno in *Catlin's Revue* at the theatre on the seafront which was called The Arcadia. In the cast were four young guys from Australia called Group One, and on the last night one of them was accused by the stage manager of putting froth into the 'Dancing Waters'! He regretted saying it was the lad, as he ended up on the floor! They were a good act, but the real 'milkers' of an audience were a double act called Earl and Elgar who, when they took their call at the end of the act, strolled off, strolled on again, and stood with their arms out to the audience for absolutely ages! However, it seemed to work! One of them was in digs with us, as was the musical director who was married to Peggy, a juggler. His first wife had not long passed away. Peggy was touring and he brought out a picture of his first wife, which was sad, but quite nice. Averill and Aurel were a very good dancing act, and Averill did lovely paintings us as a last night present, as she did for all the cast. I started courting one of the girl dancers at the other theatre, Christine, one of Rafael and his dancers. We married a couple of years later (April 1962) in Fleetwood at the Church of England on Lord Street.

Jimmy:

Touring the country and performing in every town and city is a great way to make a living. You'd meet so many great characters, and not just in the profession. There were theatrical digs in every town where there was a theatre, and they became as familiar as the stages. In Glasgow we stayed with Ma Morgan and her husband. Lovely food, the speciality being 'mince and tatties', and very tasty vegetable soup! When we played the Town Hall, Pontypridd, the landlady met us at the station and walked us to her digs. Lovely people.

In London we always stayed with Ethel Penn in Brixton: really homely digs, and always full of pros. We met some terrific people there: singers, dancers, specialty acts. One well-known double act were Eltham and Sharpe, and Billy Eltham gave us some great ideas for our act which we have used over the years. When we were there in 1954 there was also some girl dancers who were in a West End show. They told us about an eighteen year old girl singer they were with, who was fabulous. They were right – it was Shirley Bassey.

When we were playing in Luton one time, Brian and I arrived with our stage manager Al Taylor, and we got to this big old house, up on a hill. The landlady said that we had to be very quiet at nights as she had lots of working men staying there. So we went quietly to bed on that Sunday night, and then at 6 AM, all hell broke loose! Radios were blazing away, loud voices, shouting, singing! No good to us, so I had to tell the landlady it wasn't suitable. The digs in Bath were okay, but you had to pay a shilling extra if you wanted a bath! In Portsmouth there was no bathroom at all, so we had to go to the public baths to bathe!

The combined chats were the best. This was a room where you slept, lived and ate in, and it was always warm. The landlady would come in to light the fire while you were still in bed and bring your breakfast in. I had excellent digs in Borough Road, Middlesbrough, but when we arrived there was no landlady – two fellas ran the place, and it was spotless. The food was lovely too! I was very young at the time and I didn't know much about life, but I knew these chaps were different! To use an old phrase, they were as camp as a row of tents, but lovely people, and they made us really welcome.

Nowadays, of course, all the old theatrical digs have long gone. It's either a flat somewhere or a room in a Travelodge. There have been plenty of other changes along the way too. Well, there would be – we've been in the business a long time!

Through the Years...

We haven't changed that much, have we?

THE BOYS AT BUTLINS

Jimmy:

My brother and I did 12 summer seasons for Butlins as principal comedians in their revue shows. Lovely big Gaiety Theatres, big productions, great audiences. In those days we had a 12-piece theatre orchestra, and then Geraldo and his orchestra in the ballroom. Late night cabaret meant lots of stars, and we met and knew most of them. An excellent variety of different acts, too: Matt Monro, Diana Dors, Roy Castle, Ted Rogers, Jimmy Wheeler, Norman Vaughan and so many more. Bob Monkhouse was a big favourite, and so was Ken Dodd.

Our first Butlins summer season was in 1961 at Clacton on Sea. It was for Gariright Productions which was owned by Chesney Allen, of Flanagan and Allen fame. We did four seasons for them, with Bognor Regis, Minehead and Skegness after Clacton. Ches liked Brian and me, and gave us a double act routine that he used to do with Bud in the Crazy Gang shows. It was cross patter between a jockey and a trainer and was very funny. We still do the routine in different shows. Ches owned racehorses, and he liked to have a bet. In the summer of 1962 there was a brilliant racehorse called Summer Day, which won eight consecutive races. I couldn't get out to put a bet on one day when we were rehearsing, so Ches said he'd stand the bet for me. I put £30 on, which was the most money I've ever put on a horse. It won easily but the odds were 2-5 so I only got £42 back. The thrill of winning was enough for me!

Brian:

That first season at Clacton was full of comedy. We shared the billing with Colin Crompton (later becoming the Chairman at *The Wheeltappers and Shunters Social Club* on TV). Colin used to come into the theatre and throw his clothes down on the floor, put on a nice suit and light up a cigarette and would time his act with these cigarettes, smoking them on stage! He was a good comic and we did sketches and 'bits' with him and the rest of the cast. We did our hospital sketch, and of course our usual act.

We did a good number - Colin, me, Jimmy and John Killick (who became a radio DJ called Tony Brandon). John's wife was Jill Allison who was also in the show, and there were also several girl dancers. My fiancée, Christine, was also one of the dancers. They were also expected to do Redcoat duties, and had to live on the camp. She shared a chalet with a girl called Brenda, who was going out with the Redcoat comic Dave Butler, and he'd stay the night sometimes, which we weren't too happy about.

The second year that we did at Butlins was at Bognor Regis, with an old comic called Ken Roberts. He wouldn't help with our sketch but I had to feed him in his! We were asked to be with Ken the year after as well, at Minehead. When we told Ken we'd done *Sunday Night at the London Palladium*, he told us that the Palladium was "like a factory!" (Interesting, as he had only been an understudy there!) They were going to give us our own show at Minehead, topping the bill, but they said they wanted a "really good show" because they were doing a TV series from Butlins that year. It was most enjoyable although they did ask us to do matinees if inclement. Freddie "Parrot Face" Davies was the camp compere and we asked him to tell people that the show wasn't going to be on when it was sunny, on the first day of trying to perform the matinee! Guy Holloway was the company manager and he said he would perform, as did Ken Roberts, but luckily it never happened! Freddie was a good comic and a really great guy.

Jimmy:

It was in 1963 in Minehead that I met my wife Val, who was a dancer in the show. The producer was Dandy Page, and I remember him saying at rehearsals that we needed a girl in one of the comedy sketches. I said, "that gorgeous blonde would be great, wouldn't she?" That was Val, and it was the start of our romance. We were married a year later.

Brian:

In 1964 we were at Skegness topping the bill. They got a comic called Clifford Henry, whose wife kept saying, "He's usually top of the bill". We said, "Well why take the season then?" When the cheering started for him in the finale as he came down before us, we were a little astonished to see the Assistant Manager starting off the cheering for him alone. We told him to either cheer for everyone or not at all! It was fine after that. Clifford said to us that Danny Kaye had pinched his act after seeing him in Paris! We were somewhat amazed at that, and voiced our surprise!

The following year we were top of the bill at Scarborough's Spa Theatre in *Dazzle*. Eric Ross was the boss and his daughter, Brenda directed the show, which was very good. Ken Roland was a very good singer and Cecil Johnson was a good old comic. We performed in sketches with Cecil and Ken and had a lovely season.

Our lovely daughter, Julie, was born that year in the March, and when I managed to get home to see her after doing cabaret I wasn't allowed to go in to ward and visit her as it was 1 o'clock in the morning. They insisted that I wait until the following morning. My remark on seeing her was that she looked like a "little Beatle" with her fringe. Jimmy's son Lee was born that year too in the July at the hospital in Scarborough. Our son Scott was born a couple of years later and learned to play drums on a set that I bought for him. He later became a great drummer with a successful rock group called Kiss of the Gypsy. They even toured America! (He's now happily married to Diane with three great kids of his own: Thomas, Jamie and Daisy.)

Jimmy:

In 1971 we were the comics in the revue show at Butlins, Clacton-on-Sea. One of the Redcoats was a nice lad called Michael, who was very good at his job. He was always very much at ease and good with people, and the holidaymakers loved him. We used to be the guests at the donkey derby each week, handing out the rosettes to the winners. Michael always led the fun and games, and his specialty was to ride two donkeys at the same time, one leg on each, and belting around like a chariot racer from *Ben Hur.* The next time I saw him was in Selfridge's toy department when my wife and I were shopping during our season at the London Palladium. He said he was working there temporarily between engagements and that he had a cruise lined up. It was obvious he had star quality, and sure enough he made it to the top, but what a rollercoaster of a career, and a life, it proved to be for Michael Barrymore.

Many stars started off at Butlins. Another one was Freddie 'Parrot Face' Davies. We were doing the revue show at Minehead, and Freddie was the resident compere. He told us he was trying to think of something different to make a breakthrough in the business. He came up with 'Parrot Face' and "I'm sick, sick, sick up to here!" He did it on *Opportunity Knocks* for Hughie Green and that was it – stardom. He's still going strong, and has since added another string to his bow as a serious actor in films and television.

Brian and I compered the People National Talent Contest at Butlins for several years, and the same year that we met Michael Barrymore at Clacton a very funny man entered the contest, with a style all his own. He won the weekly heat easily, and the big final was the following week. He told us he was working the clubs and driving a bus to cover his costs. He asked us if we thought it was worth his while coming back for the final. We said, "Of course, you'll cake walk it!" This he did, and he went on to the big final at the London Palladium. After that came stardom on TV's *The Comedians* and much more to follow for the one and only Mike Reid. After we finished our pantomime season at the Palladium, the *Comedians* live show was the next show in. We went to see the performance and went backstage to see Mike and tell him how pleased we were with his success. He said, "What do you think of this, boys?" He'd treated himself to a big, heavy gold bracelet for £250! Not bad, eh? No more bus driving for him!

When we did a summer season at Butlins Clacton on Sea we became good friends with the ex-world snooker champion John Pullman. In our cabaret act, which we did at the theatre bar once a week, we did a comedy magic routine with half a pound of sausages and a woman volunteer from the audience. The audiences loved it and so did John! He used to come and see the show every week and bring his friends with him. He played some great exhibition matches there, like another sporting hero we met there, England test match cricketer Colin Milburn.

A good friend of ours was Wyn Calvin, the Welsh Prince of Laughter. We worked together several times over the years and he was popular with everyone. Billy Dainty played a great practical joke on him during a summer season at Butlins Skegness. Wyn was resident at Butlins for the season and Billy came to do a Sunday concert. Wyn left a note for Billy saying to use his dressing room and help himself to the chocolates and drink. His room was always well stocked up with sweets, chocolates and bottles of sherry and wine. Billy found a spare cupboard backstage and moved the whole lot and locked it away. When Wyn came back on the Monday the room was bare! Not a chocolate or drink to be seen – just a note from Billy saying, 'Thanks for the hospitality, helped myself to the refreshments, delicious!"

Brian:

For our 1972 season we were fresh from pantomime at the London Palladium. Frank Mansell gave us their top venue, so we went to Butlins at Minehead. In the show was singer Leonard Weir who'd been starring in London in *My Fair Lady* with Julie Andrews. He needed a good strong number to finish his act and we suggested he sang an old Josef Locke number called 'Goodbye'. We also suggested that he swing his coat at the end of number, which went down really well with the audience. He thanked us for the idea.

1973 took us to Filey, for a very enjoyable season. We were the comics and there were times when we had to clear the theatre because of bomb threats! Jimmy and I would come off stage, grab our main belongings and props and go outside for as long as it took to make the place safe! Not a very clever thing to have to do with a full audience, but that's what was happening at that time. Tony Peers was the resident Butlins compere up there, and he did a very good job. For 1974 we were in Jersey, in Dick Ray's "Excitement" show. This was a touring show, which toured the hotels all season. We were the comics and had a great season, even though our digs had fleas, which meant that the rooms had to be fumigated.

In 1977 we were in summer season at the Babbacombe Theatre, Torquay. We had a lovely season but unfortunately my marriage to Christine was now in trouble and the holidays weren't as happy as I had hoped. Once the season was finished it was clear that our marriage was as good as over as she had obviously fallen out of love with me and had found someone else.

Jimmy:

At Babbacombe we appeared with Billy Burden, a very funny yokel comedian and a good friend. It's a nice little theatre but only a couple of the dressing rooms had sinks. Brian and I had a sink in our room but Billy didn't. We were just getting ready for the show and putting on our make-up one night when Billy walked in. He said, "Do you mind if I use your sink, lads?" We said, "No, of course not, be our guest." We expected him to wash his hands and face, but no. He dropped his trousers and underpants and started to wash his backside. Then he calmly dried himself and, with a 'Thanks, lads!" off he went.

Brian:

I had time to reflect and move on and I was definitely not going to get married again, and was going to 'play the field' as I was in my forties... so it was a case of open shirt, medallion, curly perm and sports car! My younger brother Paul asked me to share his house, and I was given an upstairs room in Greaseborough. (It has since been condemned and knocked down!) I shared the house with two dogs that disgraced themselves on my landing and stairs on many occasions. The puppy was unfortunately killed on the road outside the house, and Paul in tears asked me to bury it. I did, and then the older dog dug it up! We had to bury it again, but deeper. Then the older dog left more 'presents' on a regular basis, and as I was the first one up in the house it seemed to be my job to get rid of these offerings. Lucky me! But my swinging bachelor days soon came to an end, in any event.

We didn't have a season pencilled in for 1983, and at the last minute Duggie Chapman decided to take over the Gaiety Theatre in the Isle of Man. It was a good show and we enjoyed the time over there. My digs were at a farmhouse out in the country. The good thing was that we got fresh eggs every morning because when the chickens layed, they clucked loudly, and the eggs were still warm. The bad thing was the telephone, which was in a dark secluded little outhouse in the pitch black and outside. I'd met my wife Rachel by this time and I used to phone her every night (she was in the Black and White Minstrel show in Eastbourne for the season). She had to pick up the phone almost before it rang so as not to wake her landlord and landlady who had to get up really early each morning. Rachel and I were married in the autumn of 1983 in Rotherham, and then had a lovely church blessing in Maltby. Our honeymoon was three days in Ilkley before we had to be in Norwich for pantomime publicity!

THE BOYS ON THE BOX

Jimmy:

There's no denying the power of television. I remember back in the sixties we did cabaret in Liverpool. It was a big ballroom and the place was packed. They were all eating and drinking when the cabaret started: we opened up, and got nowhere. Then Cleo Laine and Johnny Dankworth came on. Nobody listened! Next up was Harry Worth. We thought, "Oh no, poor old Harry!" They were all still talking, and he was a very quiet comedian. But as soon as his name was announced everybody shut up, they cheered when he came on and he tore 'em up. They loved him! And why? Well, he was very funny, but the deciding factor was that he had just been a big hit on TV on the Royal Variety Performance. And that's the power of television!

Brian:

At rehearsals Cleo and Johnny kept going on and on, while we waited for our turn. I had to keep moving my car as it was on a half hour parking spot. Eventually we said, "Will you be long, as we are here to rehearse?" They apologised, saying how sorry they were, but had thought that we were a couple of waiters! Very nice!

Jimmy:

Our first ever television appearance was in 1957 in a BBC talent show called *It's Up To You*. It was produced by Barney Colehan and was like *Opportunity Knocks* where the viewers had to vote by writing in. There were six acts on each week and the winners came back the following week to chat to the presenter and collect their prize. Several stars, including Ted Rogers and the Pinky and Perky puppet act, got their big break on the programme.

Brian:

There were some good acts performing on the programme, including Harry Shields, a good comedian who told us he was liable to win it, as he had just done pantomime and they were all going to vote for him! The compere was Peter West who was a very well-known TV presenter. There was a panel of judges who gave their idea of who they thought would win each week. We won by a mile! We were thrilled, of course, and Barney Colehan used us in a lot of his BBC live shows after that. We were asked to return the following week as winners and asked what we would like for a prize. We asked for "two new suits and a script by the script-writers for Morecambe and Wise!"

Jimmy:

The first big show we did on BBC TV was in 1958. It was a spectacular production called *Hit the Headlines.* It was the story of a newspaper office and the stars were Terry-Thomas, Dickie Valentine, Jill Day and Jeremy Hawk. Jill looked beautiful – I had been a fan of hers for a long time! Brian and I played copy boys in the office and we did a song and dance routine with Dickie Valentine to 'Top Hat, White Tie and Tails', and also in the show was Irving Davies, who was a great dancer and choreographer. Terry-Thomas had a new joke to tell us every day at rehearsal.

Brian:

In one scene I had to take a live pigeon from a small cage and take it to Terry-Thomas. He had to say to me that there was a message from our foreign correspondent and I was to go and get it. I then had to go and fetch the message from the bird. The first time I tried this I put my hand in the cage, took hold of the bird and missed one wing, so it flapped about aimlessly!! Luckily on the live broadcast I got the 'message' with no problem and handed the bird to Terry without any problems!

Jimmy:

We were at the Edinburgh Palladium when rehearsals started, and we finished our show at about 10.30 on the Saturday night. We were due at the rehearsal rooms at Shepherd's Bush in London at 9.30 am the following morning! I had just bought my first car then. In fact it was a Thames Van. Brand new, it was dark green, but I had it sprayed pink. I thought it looked superb... It was certainly different! Anyway, Brian and I drove non-stop through the night from Edinburgh right down the A1 to London. We took it in turns driving while the other one had a kip in the back of the van. The police stopped us once, and warned us that the limit was 50mph in a van. We apologised and explained that we had to be in London for our TV show. They let us off with a warning but if we had stuck to that limit we'd never have made it there in time. We were shattered through lack of sleep but nevertheless we staggered into the rehearsal room and met the producer, Francis Essex, and all the stars. Terry-Thomas looked very dapper, as always, and had a new joke to tell every day. We had quite a few lines to learn, as well as our routine with Dickie Valentine, and it was a really pleasurable experience. All television was live at that time, so it was much more exciting to do than a recorded show.

Speaking of the police just then, I must mention the most exciting car ride I've ever been on. We were in pantomime at the Gaiety Theatre in Dublin, as Captain and mate. We finished our dress rehearsal at about 10.30pm, and were due to appear live on Teilifís Éireann on the *Late Late Show* with Gay Byrne at about 11 o'clock. We dashed out of the stage door in full costume and make-up, and there was a taxi waiting with two police motorcycle escorts. It was a few miles at the other side of the city, and I just couldn't believe it. We were doing at least 90 mph following the two outriders with their sirens blaring, going through red traffic lights and even driving on the wrong side of the road at times. Exhilarating stuff, and we made it to the studio with white knuckles and time to spare!

Brian:

When we did Val Parnell's *Star Time* for ATV, Alma Cogan was the star of the show. She had asked especially for Jimmy and me after being on *Be My Guest* with us a week or so before, which was most flattering. Also on the bill was Jack Douglas, who at that time was part of a comedy double act, and had just signed a contract for TV. We did our spot for the cameras and Alma was watching with Jack, who said something to her, obviously about us doing comedy in the show. We finished our spot, and the director said, "We're running short of time, so just do the song and dance, which is great!" We knew what Douglas must have said. Years later he wanted to use my house in Fleetwood to stay in during summer season at Blackpool Pier. I said no! Joe Church had it instead! *All Kinds of Music* for ATV was another brilliant show, but we followed Tubby Hayes who was a jazz saxophonist. Great stuff, but the end of his number was a solo that went on and on and on, and our lead-in followed it! We kept thinking, is he ever going to finish? We were on standby for what seemed like an eternity!

Jimmy:

Appearing on TV is very different from stage work. When we did *Seaside Special* for the BBC we filmed it in a huge marquee, and the dressing rooms were small caravans. But the one TV show that was exactly like working on stage was, of course, *The Good Old Days.* It was a fabulous show to appear in and Brian and I appeared on five occasions. There aren't many dressing rooms at the famous Leeds City Varieties, so we all had to share. On one occasion we shared a room with the American entertainer Stubby Kaye from *Guys and Dolls*, and I remember him wearing boxer shorts and it seeming strange to us as we'd never heard of them over here in those days. (He also had a strange new deodorant from America... called Old Spice!)

Another time, Donald Peers was the star singing his signature tune 'In a Shady Nook by a Babbling Brook'. The act before him did a slapstick routine that finished up with a huge cream cake in the face. They decided to save the cake for the actual performance and just mimed it during rehearsals. Well, come the show and *slap*! This huge cream cake hit the stooge in the face and splattered all over the stage. Panic stations! As compere Leonard Sachs announced Donald they got Albert, the character that always appeared on the show, to go on with a broom and try to sweep it up. But although he did his best it was like a skating rink. Poor Donald Peers came on, looking immaculate, and in seconds he was slipping all over the place, with cream on his shoes and over his trousers. The whole show had to be stopped and redone. Oh dear!

The City of Varieties has a lovely atmosphere and looks wonderful on TV, but backstage it really is ancient and derelict. I used a real sandwich in our act there and after the show I left the sandwich in my pocket and hung my coat up on a hanger on the wall. When I came into the dressing room the next day my coat was still on the wall, but with a big hole where a rat had nibbled right through the coat and into the sandwich in my pocket! How it managed to get up there and eat the bread I will never know. It must have hung on as it nibbled away!

Another show with a live stage atmosphere was ITV's *Wheeltappers and Shunters Social Club.* The resident stars were Bernard Manning and Colin Crompton and they filmed two programmes at the same time, so there were twice as many acts as you would normally see. We were on with Bill Haley and the Comets, Marty Wilde, the Three Degrees and several others. The Three Degrees were making their first appearance in England, and somehow we got sent their contract by mistake. No one knew them then so they were earning peanuts! In no time they shot to stardom and were earning thousands.

Brian:

I got to see another side of TV over the years, as I've often appeared as a walk-on artist in the gaps between summer seasons and pantomimes, and touring in *Chucklevision*. I was a bus conductor and plenty of other things in *Eastenders*, as well as appearing in *Holby City, By the Sword Divided, CATS Eyes,* and *Lost Empires* with Laurence Olivier and Colin Firth, among many others. I also did walk-ons in Bruce Forsyth's sitcom *Slinger's Day*, and on *The Generation Game.* We'd worked with Bruce on a charity Sunday concert at Plymouth, and met him again when we were at Manchester Palace with Ronnie Corbett, but he didn't seem to remember me!

I appeared many times in *The Bill*, including as a dead body. When they shouted "Turn over!" to the crew, I thought, "should I?" They also filmed me in a hospital mortuary as a dead body on a trolley. When we heard a shout of "There's a real body coming in!" I was asked to vacate the trolley! (The programme eventually had its own hospital set to avoid such incidents!) At one stage I was the resident drunk for the series, appearing several times in that incapacitated capacity!

DOING THE ROUNDS

Jimmy:

A panto in winter and a good summer season left us with spring and autumn to tour the clubs. On Sunday it was noon and night. At dinner time from 12 noon to 2pm we'd have to do three spots of about fifteen minutes each to an audience of men. Sometimes they were hard, but usually we did all right. If they didn't like our comedy we had our songs and our fast tap dancing routines which always went well. The concert secretary would say, "They'll be better tonight when the women are in!" They'd all come in with their wives and we'd do four spots (two either side of the bingo). It was always better at night.

Some of the concert secretaries were real characters. This is how we were introduced at the British Legion Club, somewhere in Doncaster:

"Ladies and gentlemen, as you probably know, one of our members, Bert Johnson, passed away on Tuesday night. He was a very popular member of our club and I know he'll be missed by every one of us here. Can we now have two minutes silence?"

And then, after the two minutes passed:

"And now, here to entertain you are the Patton Brothers!"

Can you imagine? They were all crying into their beers and we had to go on and try to get laughs! Sometimes in the middle of your act the bell would ring and they'd announce that the pies and peas were ready at the back. We used to love it when the bingo went on longer than usual and they'd say, "You don't have to go on again!"

When we did our act at the Regency Club, Widnes, we were told that there were lots of rugby players in the area and that there were always fights on Friday nights. Sure enough, while Brian and I were halfway through our act and singing 'Side by Side' – crash, bang, wallop – a big fight starts up right at the back of the club. People kept turning around to see what was happening but we just kept on singing and dancing. We got off as quick as we could, and that was that!

For several summer seasons I was compere at Haggerston Castle Holiday Park, Berwick Upon Tweed. On a Saturday night I'd do a warm-up spot to welcome everyone and do a good old singalong. It was halfway between Newcastle and Edinburgh, so the audience consisted of Geordies and Scots. So to finish up I'd do 'Blaydon Races' to get the Geordies singing and 'Donald, Where's Your Trewsers' for the Scots. The general manager stopped me doing it because he said it caused fights, and certainly that was true on occasions, when half the audience would sing 'Flower of Scotland' and get the Geordies mad!

I used to hate going on late in a club when they were all sozzled. I remember one night at a holiday camp in Scarborough. Ronnie Hilton was top of the bill and we were the supporting act. We were supposed to go on at eight o'clock and then Ronnie at midnight. He was a pal of ours and he said, "Do you mind swapping, boys? I don't fancy going on late." Well we obliged, but by that time they were all noisy and drunk. So we said, "Forget the patter, nobody's listening!" We dug out an old singalong routine, and they loved that. We got one half of the audience to sing 'Pack Up Your Troubles' and the other half to sing 'It's a Long Way to Tipperary', separately and then at the same time. They actually go together perfectly! After that, we finished with a fast song and dance routine: loud and noisy and just what they wanted at that time of night. Then you'd get just the opposite: you'd arrive early at a club and the concert secretary would say, "Are you gonna get us started, then?" with about 25 people in. Then at the end he'd say, "Do as long as you want this time." Marvellous!

One time when we were filming Ronnie Corbett's Saturday special on BBC TV, we went into the BBC canteen with Ronnie for dinner. Everywhere you looked there were familiar faces. Joan Sims was next to me in the queue and gave me a nice smile. Tony Booth asked me where the gents was! Every table had a star sitting at it. To my left were Ronnie Barker and the *Porridge* cast. To my right were Larry Grayson and Isla St. Clair. Right next to us were Peter Cushing, Vincent Price, Gayle Hunnicut and Lee Remick. I had been a keen autograph collector as a lad – well this was an autograph hunter's dream come true!

We've always enjoyed meeting, and sometimes working with all the straight actors. It's a wonderful profession because actors respect and enjoy our side of the profession as much as we respect and enjoy the serious acting side. Often, you get to see a whole new side of them. I remember meeting the celebrated actor Edward Hardwicke when we were doing a Sunday concert at the Babbacombe Theatre, Torquay. He was the son of the great Hollywood star Sir Cedric Hardwicke, and later on he was wonderful as Doctor Watson to Jeremy Brett's Sherlock Holmes. Ronnie Corbett rang up to say that he and his wife Ann would like to come and see the show that night. They were on holiday with Edward and his wife, and all of four of them would be coming. I arranged complimentary tickets and they all came and really enjoyed the show. We'd known Ronnie and Ann for years, but had never met Edward. We expected the dapper actor to come backstage in in a smart suit, but he was wearing wellington boots and a pack-a-mac! They were on a camping holiday together, and the tent site was muddy. Nevertheless, it was lovely to meet him.

On one matinee performance of *Cinderella* at the Palladium we could see Susan George in the audience, and she looked beautiful. You could see that lovely smile from several rows back in the stalls. Malcolm Roberts, who was playing the Prince, offered to introduce us, as he knew we were big fans of hers. Sure enough there was a tap on our door in between shows, and she was delightful. She came in and chatted to us like we were old pals. She was really natural and friendly, and just as you'd hope a star like her would be.

Brian:

In 1959 we were appearing live on BBCTV on the *Joan Regan Show*. She was a bubbly blonde girl with an attractive voice and a lovely face. We were ready and waiting for Joan to introduce us, when we realised that standing right next to us on the set was Cary Grant! Apparently he was there to see Alma Cogan, who was also a guest on the show. He smiled and said good luck, and we were on! We saw him again when we did pantomime at the Hippodrome, Bristol, and he came to see the show with his mother.

Jimmy and I have always got a thrill from seeing the great actors. When we were doing a season at the Palladium in Edinburgh we loved to go to see the plays at the King's Theatre. Some excellent stars appeared there, including Claire Bloom, Flora Robson and Albert Finney. We saw the beautiful Vivien Leigh there in *Duel of Angels*. She was of course the wife of the great Laurence Olivier, who Jimmy and I had the pleasure of working with in the TV series *Lost Empires* (which was about Moss Empires). I'll never forget the time the great Laurence came and sat out front in front of us. Someone said, "Good morning, Lord Olivier". Someone else said the same, as we did. He replied with that wonderful voice saying: "Sorry, I can't get my f***ing head round any further!" We all fell about! A wonderful actor and it was magic to say that we had worked with him.

One day in Edinburgh, as we were waiting to go in, Charles Laughton and Elsa Lanchester came walking up to the stage door. I had my cine camera with him and we asked politely if Mr Laughton minded me filming him as he was walking up to the theatre with his wife. He gave me a nice smile and kindly agreed – a great moment, and I treasure my film. The fabulous Bela Lugosi I got to see in *Dracula* way back in 1950 when I was with Billy West's Harmony Boys, again in Edinburgh. He was on at the Lyceum. I remember him appearing through a cloud of dry ice to wild applause. Magic to see!

Jimmy:

Actors with a reputation for drama often like to show that they can do knockabout comedy. Paul Henry is best remembered as Benny in *Crossroads*, but he was excellent in panto at the Theatre Royal, Norwich. He had a go at everything! The boss, Dick Condon, told us that Paul was an actor but he could adapt to anything, and asked if we could suggest any comedy routines that we could use Paul in. We did, and he was great in them. We did a number where he sang while we dressed him up in a kilt, red beard and paint brush sporran, our ice cream routine, with lots of splosh and slapstick and a high wire routine where we were three acrobats, and Paul was on a wire and we threw him all over the place. He also did a bathroom scene where he got absolutely drenched at every performance. He was a big success and he deserved it. He liked a little flutter and one night he took me to the casino in Great Yarmouth. I said I couldn't really afford to go as I wasn't earning big money, but he insisted and gave me £20 to gamble with. (That was a nice bit of money in 1983.) He was a very generous lad and good company. I was lucky at first playing roulette, but after about an hour I just had the £20 left, so I gave it back to Paul.

Then I remember an evening performance of *Dick Whittington* at the Gaiety Theatre, Dublin in February, 1991. Just as we were about to start, somebody said: "Oliver Reed is in the audience!" Sure enough, there he was in the fourth row of the stalls with his young wife. He was wearing a striped rugby shirt and we could see him clearly. When the interval came we thought that would probably be the last we'd see of him – he'll go for a drink at the bar and stay there! But no, when the curtain went up he was there in his seat again. The bar lady told us later that as soon as the bell went for the start of the second half he said, "I must go now. I'm really enjoying the show."

He came into the green room after the show and that's where we met him. He was great to talk to and very interesting. Brian and I are both ardent filmgoers and we'd always followed his career. We chatted to him for ages about his films and all the people he'd worked with. He asked us what we'd like to drink and, being a teetotaller, I asked for lemonade. He fetched the drinks without flinching which just shows what a gentleman he was. With him being a renowned hard drinker one might think that he'd expect everyone in his company to be the same. But no, he was totally charming and the complete opposite of the hair-raising stories you'd read about him. He told us he wished he'd done pantomime. He would have been great as the villain.

Brian:

Ollie also told us he didn't get on with Amanda Donohoe during the filming of *Castaway*, and ended up slightly drunk. We were told that by the end of the evening he was playing a game of 'who could spit the farthest' in the bar!

Jimmy:

After our season at the Palladium – we'll come to that in a bit! - we were offered three months in the Bahamas in cabaret, followed by a month in Las Vegas. We turned it down because we were hoping to make a name here. Also, we both had young families and didn't want to leave them for that length of time. Nonetheless, we have often played in other countries, and it was always an enjoyable and eye-opening experience.

In 1959 we were the comics on a Combined Services Entertainments tour of Aden, Bahrain and Cyprus. Another show touring there was headed by Ruby Murray and Hal Roach. We all stayed at the Ledra Palace Hotel in Nicosia and used to have table tennis competitions there. We didn't meet Ruby again until 1987 when we were in summer season for Bourne Leisure at Rockley Sands, Poole in Dorset. There was a young singer with the band called Tim Burgess and he was very good. We discovered that he was

Ruby's son by her first husband, Bernie Burgess of the Jones Boys. One night during the season she came to see the show, and we introduced her to the audience. They loved her and they were all asking for her autograph and taking photos – once a star, always a star!

We did one show in the Persian Gulf, and the lads had built a wooden stage for us. Well, the opening of the show was the whole company singing 'Get Happy' and then going into a dance routine. We did the first step, and both of us went right through the stage. It stopped the show and the lads loved it. The only snag was that for the next two hours we had to do the whole show working around the big hole in the stage.

By way of contrast, in 1966 we did a TV show in Hanover, Germany, and there was a marvellous 40-piece orchestra to accompany us, the Nord Deutsch Rundfunk. What a thrill to hear that music! They wrote and asked us for band parts, and of course we'd been playing variety theatres that usually had an 8-piece band! However, we'd done *The Good Old Days* on BBC TV with the Northern Dance Orchestra who had augmented our parts, so they got the rest of the music required from them.

Brian:

The show was called *Einer Wird Gewinnen*, which means 'Everyone a Winner'. Hanover was lovely and the studio was right by the river. We'd got the train over there, and having seen all the British war movies, it was rather frightening to hear "Achtung, Achtung!" from the ticket collectors on the train.

We were paid in franks and marks over the counter! Top of the bill were the New Christie Minstrels. Their roadie was a great guy who had been part of a double dancing act called The Condos Brothers who Dad had known of in the business. He loved our act and we have seen The Condos Brothers' act and they were great.

Jimmy:

We had an enjoyable tour of South Africa in 1973 with the Cilla Black show. It was an excellent show and for six weeks we appeared in Capetown, Johannesburg, Durban and Pretoria. People often ask us what Cilla was like, and I can honestly say that I don't know. She stayed in big hotels while the rest of us stayed in apartments, and was taken everywhere in limousines while we were in a mini-bus. The president of South Africa, Dr Foucha, came to see the show and afterwards we all lined up to meet him on stage. Cilla stayed in her room and the president had to go in there to see her. We didn't actually get to speak to her until the very last night of the tour, and she was very nice.

Brian:

Apartheid was on and we had to do a separate show for black audiences, who came dressed up to the nines and were great. We met 'Miss Africa South', a lovely black girl who we were introduced to by a great black reporter. The black people had their own bus – we tried to get on once, and they shouted at us to get off! We couldn't use the Gents with them either. Coming back on the plane, Kenny Lynch was on our flight, and he used a whites only phone box, and a South African woman told him to come out of the box! I won't tell you what he said to her, but it ended in "off"! Kenny was a great guy.

Also on the bill were three great Spanish lads and a fabulous dance act called Augie and Margo. They had worked with Sammy Davis on tour in America and they told us that Sammy did brilliantly at one place and was bragging, "I did better than Frank" just as Frank Sinatra walked into the dressing room! The band were on stage with us, and we loved hearing Cilla sing 'Alfie'. She gave us a drink at the end of the tour, and Bobby, her husband, used to chat to us about Liverpool Football club.

On the first morning in Cape Town we went down to breakfast in our hotel, and on the patio one of the Quibell brothers, who put the show on, introduced us to a film actress sitting there by saying, "This is Mary Ann Fields". We said "Shirley!" She said "Thank you!"

Jimmy:

She looked gorgeous and we chatted about the flight and the lovely country we were in. She flew to Johannesburg the next day, and I didn't see her again until I went to see her in the play *Absent Friends* in the summer of 1997. After 24 years, she was a beautiful as ever.

Jerry Stevens was compere and he did a great job. He managed to get a free car wherever he went as long as he gave their company a plug on stage. He took us out on some lovely outings too. Unfortunately we had some bad luck when we were in Durban. We drove out to the Valley of a Thousand Hills to see the Zulu settlements: breathtaking scenery, and a wonderful experience. We parked the car and strolled forward to look at the view when some chap in a mini-van full of tourists reversed back without looking into his mirror. He went straight into Jerry's car, puncturing the radiator and making a right mess of the bodywork. Water was pouring out quite steadily. We had to get back for the show that night and it was a fair distance away! There was no time to wait for help, so Jerry would drive a few miles with steam pouring out of the engine, then stop and fill up with water, carry on a few more miles, then repeat the procedure. We were lucky the radiator didn't' burst completely, but we made it back eventually. The car hire company was very good about it and just gave him another car.

I love traveling abroad because I'm a sun worshipper, but there's just one problem – the food! I usually eat the soup and the dessert and that's it! I returned to Sri Lanka where I had done my national service in 1994 and it was wonderful, just as if time had stood still. It brought back so many lovely memories. In our hotel one night they laid on the most lavish banquet you could wish for, all laid out buffet style. There was every exotic dish you can imagine, and people were piling up their plates with huge helpings. I'd been wandering around for ages, and all I had on my plate was a tomato and piece of beetroot. The Sri Lankan chef looked at me and said, "You no like my food?" I told him I didn't like anything spicy, or hot, or with garlic. He made my day when he said, "I cook you omelette and French fries!" Fantastic!

Mind you, sometimes being fussy about food helps you out. One memorable engagement was when Brian and I were booked to do one half hour cabaret spot on a Thursday evening in Torremolinos, with a week's holiday thrown in free. Our wives came free, too! When we got there the resident entertainment's team had all got the Torremolinos Trots! They were all ill, but carried on with the show like real troopers. There was a bucket by the piano for emergencies, and they told the audience they should be wearing brown trousers instead of white. I was fine!

GOOD COMPANIONS

Jimmy:

I remember a Variety Club Luncheon at the Midland Hotel in Manchester that was full of great pros. Les Dawson, Russ Abbot, John Inman and Dora Bryan were on the main table. The rest of the room was full of entertainers from all walks of the profession. There were speeches from the stars, and then the compere Kevin Kent introduced artists from each table who stood up and took a bow. Kevin gave us a lovely introduction, saying: "Here are two lads who have been in the business all their lives. They're not stars but they always do a great act and are respected throughout the profession. It's a pleasure to introduce the Patton Brothers." We got a lovely reception, as we either knew or had worked with nearly everyone there.

We've met some wonderful people in this business over the years, and the bigger the star the nicer they seemed to be. When we appeared on Russ Conway's show on ITV, Morecambe and Wise were also on the bill. I used to wear a turned-up trilby doing the comedy business, and I remember Eric telling us that he used to wear one like that too. We had a lovely chat and when he left he said, "Keep up the good work, lads." Eric and Ernie were big stars, of course, but they went out of their way to be nice to us.

Brian:

We loved Eric and Ernie and they always sent us their regards. On the Russ Conway show we mentioned that we were doing pantomime for Derek Salburg at the Alexandra Theatre in Birmingham. Eric said, "Derek would come up to us and say 'Why do you do that little joke early in your act?', and we said 'It gets a titter and we like doing it', which threw him a little". Eric said that on Saturday nights he and Ernie used to dash away home to the wives and for some reason Derek threw a party in the bar with drinks that night. He wasn't wildly happy, but it was something he did every week. He later changed it to Friday nights, which is what it was when

Jimmy and I were there. Great comics and great guys. They certainly left their mark in the business.

Jimmy:

One of the nicest men you could ever meet was the late Leslie Crowther. We did three pantomime seasons with Leslie, from 1974 to 1977. Leslie loved cricket, and he took us to Trent Bridge for a tour of everything and a practice in the nets. He was excellent in pantomime and hilarious offstage. Wherever he was, he'd have us in stitches. At the Lord Mayor's reception in Nottingham he'd suddenly put a flat cap on, shove a cigarette up his nose, scratch his backside and say, "By gum, nice little place here isn't it, my duck?" in a broad Midlands accent! Everybody loved him. He was such a genuinely nice person. We had three coachloads of friends and relations come to the pantomime, and we asked Leslie if he'd pop out after the show just to say a quick hello. He boarded each coach, shook hands with everyone, told jokes, and spent about twenty minutes of his valuable time with our friends. That's the type of man he was. A real gem.

John Inman was like that too. There are some stars who creep out of the theatre and avoid all their fans, leaving them waiting in vain. John would sit in the stage manager's office by the stage door and sign everyone's autograph for as long as it took. He was a lovely man and great company. We had been friends since we worked together at the Bristol Hippodrome in 1972. John was one of the ugly sisters with Barry Howard, another very good performer. It was while we were there that John got his big break as Mr Humphreys in *Are You Being Served?* One of the biggest laughs I've ever had was at the last night party on stage at the Palace, Manchester. John and Barry had both had a few, and they were dressed in smart suits and looked very dapper. In the panto they did a strip routine, and at the party the band suddenly struck up with the *Stripper* music. What followed was hilarious – I've never laughed so much. We all thought they'd stop at the trousers coming off, but no: it all came off!

Which reminds me of the first time I met Ray Alan in 1957, when we did a season together at the Ampitheatre, Rhyl. It was only a small theatre so all the men shared one dressing room and the girls shared the other. We did six changes of programme, which meant that we did a different show every night. You can imagine how many costumes and props were hanging up. Ray was a brilliant ventriloquist – even when you were stood right next to him, you couldn't see his mouth move at all. He was excellent in sketches too as the dapper straight man, and he played the uke as well! But his *piece de resistance* was shown to us in the dressing room. All the lads were there, and he suddenly said: "Here's my impression of a duck in flight!" He stripped completely, dropped his underpants and manipulated his wedding tackle – and there was the funniest sight you've ever seen.

Brian:

We first worked with the Bachelors when they weren't even called the Bachelors – they were called the Harmonichords, of all things! It was in Dublin in cabaret. Then Jimmy and I did a BBC show in Bristol fronted by singer Jimmy Young, and the three lads were on it with singer Jackie Trent, among others. The agent in Dublin at the time was an old lad called Percy

Holmshawe, who had a strange habit of lighting up a cigar as you entered his offices, which he then never seemed to smoke. We got a laugh when Con and Dec came in to see us in pantomime at Wolverhampton, when as the Robbers we crept in to the Babes' room in the dark, and I said, "This looks like Percy Holmeshawe's office!"

Jimmy:

Ted Rogers was a pal since we did *Robinson Crusoe* at the Grand, Leeds, in 1965/6, with Ronnie Hilton and Jack Tripp. In that show there were two comedy ballets. Ted had it in his contract that he must do a comedy ballet, and Jack had it written in his contract too. So after the usual ballet with the fairy we then had two comedy ballets – the only time I can ever remember that happening. Ted was one of the most topical comedians in the business. I remember when we went to see him at the Palladium where he was supporting Tom Jones. We were sitting in his dressing room with the show due to start, and he had the news on his TV set. His gag writer Wally was there with pencil and paper, and an item about Prince Charles came on. Wally said, "I've got a good line you can use about this, Ted – you can do it second house. Can't use it first house because that audience won't have seen the news item." Now that's topical!

We did *Cinderella* with Ted at the Pavilion, Bournemouth, and in his first entrance he used to throw out presents to the audience. This included a packet of sausages, which hit a woman in the face at one performance! The other snag was that the kids used to throw some of the presents back, and the orchestra members were not amused! They'd all disappear from the pit and huddle up against the front of the stage, but the trumpeter was hit once and we never heard the last of it.

Brian:

We loved working with Ted. We even did our song 'We Ain't Going Nowhere' with him, when he asked us if he could sing it too, as he loved it so much. His kind of number, all wordy! We also worked with Ted in the early sixties on the BBC TV series *Club Night*, filmed in Manchester. The compere was singer Donald Peers (famous for 'In a Shady Nook by a Babbling Brook'). We decided to do something different, so we performed as two stars from *Z-Cars* tap dancing, as well as other TV duos, doing the same sort of thing. Ted said it was a good spot. He was worried because warming up the audience was a well-known gay comic who was starring at the club that we were filming in. Obviously Ted couldn't do 'naughty' material, whereas the warm up comic could! Ted's act went really well though, and the audience loved his material. We still miss Ted, but had the great pleasure of working with his son Danny in pantomime in 2016 at Port Sunlight. A lovely lad. Ted would be so proud of him.

Danny La Rue came in to see the pantomime we did with Ronnie Corbett at the London Palladium, and we heard that he wanted us for pantomime with him at Manchester Palace. We couldn't do it, as we went with Ronnie to Bristol, but we got to work with him in Duggie Chapman's Old Time Music Hall, where we were guest stars. He used to ask things of us like, "could you open the window" in the dressing room! The first night we toured he brought in a great comedy audience and we went down great. We came off stage and Dan said "Marvellous!", and we thought how nice of him to say so. However, he followed that statement with, "exactly twenty minutes!" (which took the shine off it a little!) We toured with him later, and one night Dan was late for some reason. The curtain was held for about half an hour, and so that the audience wouldn't grumble, Dan bought the whole audience a cup of tea. Such a nice thing to do. Although the artistes and crew weren't part of that generosity, so we didn't get one!

Jimmy:

Ken Dodd is one of the funniest men around and he's just as funny offstage. We did some sketches with him on his BBC TV show. One was a cross between *Opportunity Knocks* and *New Faces* called *New Knockers*. Brian and I were dressed up as two Nazi SS men in full uniform and jackboots and we did a fast tap routine to the German national anthem! We also worked the Wakefield Theatre Club with Ken, and the Winter Gardens, Morecambe. A two hour cabaret spot is nothing for Ken. We were doing a season at Butlins, Filey in 1973 and went to see him do a late night cabaret. Late was the operative word! It was 2.30 before he finished, but nobody complained. The roars just kept coming. He was tremendous.

Brian:

We did a couple of TV shows with Doddy, including one where we had to get a third person who needed to be the same size as us, so we enrolled brother Paul (who wasn't a name in those days). We did one part as three dancing male chauvinist pigs in full evening dress with pigs' heads, singing and dancing to 'Give Me the Moonlight'! I bumped into Paul at one stage accidentally, and Doddy said "That's the taxi driver bumping!" (Paul was currently driving his own taxi at the time!) We also did a short sketch with Faith Brown, where we were all sitting in bed together. The shot showed Doddy saying, "Good night, dear", then Faith saying "Good night", then cut to Jimmy doing the same, then me, and then Paul, all in the same bed!

Jimmy:

One of the best double acts I've ever worked with was Sid and Max Harrison who were a big name in the forties: great eccentric comics and very funny men. I was with the Dead End Kids in variety at the Preston Hippodrome and they were top of the bill. On the Friday night we did a radio broadcast live from the theatre and everybody did something. Sid and Max kept the whole evening going and did five different comedy routines, all brilliant. In one they were a jockey and his trainer, in another two gangsters, in another two convicts. In 1946 the Kids shared the bill with Dick Henderson, a very popular North Country comedian. Everyone remembers his son Dickie Henderson, who was also a terrific entertainer of course. I worked with him too, and had the pleasure of telling him I'd also appeared with his dad at the Empire West, Hartlepool. Us lads were in the dressing room next to him, and we had all our make-up boxes and props and everything else laid out all over the dressing room table. Dick's room was empty apart from one bowler hat and one cigar. He'd walk into the theatre about ten minutes before he was due to go on stage. Then he would go into his dressing room, put on the bowler, light up the cigar, walk on and do his act!

One of the best things about those early days was getting to see the real comedy greats. When we were in the revue *Honky Tonk* at the Palace Theatre, Reading in 1955, the one and only Max Miller made a guest appearance one night. He was a friend of Bob Grey, the boss of our show, and lived nearby. What a thrill to see such a comedy legend perform. He did a great spot in his white suit and trilby hat, leaning over the footlights to chat to the audience. I also worked several times with one of the Crazy Gang, 'Monsewer' Eddie Gray. He was one of the world's greatest practical jokers. One time he was sharing a dressing room with a chap who said, "Listen, Eddie, I've got this new girlfriend coming to the show tonight. She's very quiet and comes from a very good family – please, no practical jokes!" Well, that evening this lad was in the dressing room with his girlfriend when there was a tap at the door. In walks Eddie, stark naked except for a top hat and bow tie. He walks up to the sink, has a pee in it, lifts his hat to the girl and says: "Good evening", and then walks out. Follow that!

Tommy Trinder was another of the all-time greats and terrific company. We used to do Sunday concerts at Butlins and we all had a meal together after the show. We'd sit there for hours enjoying Tommy's anecdotes and reminiscences. We also shared a love of football. The last time we worked with Tommy was in music hall at the Civic Theatre, Rotherham. He'd done his act and the audience loved him. We were all on stage doing the finale and I was standing next to Tommy. Suddenly he collapsed and fell to the floor just as the tabs came down. He'd fainted and was out for ages. We were all very worried and he was rushed to hospital. The next day Brian and I visited him and he was sitting up and quite chirpy. But the doctor said he had to rest so he went back to London and didn't appear in the show for the rest of the week.

Brian:

When we first saw his lovely car outside The Gaiety, Clacton, we saw 'TT' and thought it was Terry-Thomas! He was a great comic, who was known as the greatest putter-down of hecklers. Unfortunately when he was top of the bill at the Civic Rotherham with us, he was quite deaf so couldn't hear what the hecklers were shouting, and it threw him! Lovely guy, Tommy.

Jimmy:

In show business you don't see friends for years and years sometimes, but when you do meet again it's as if you've never been away. We're a different breed somehow, and there's always something to talk about. We first met Engelbert Humperdinck when we worked together at the Scala Club in Doncaster. He was known as Gerry Dorsey then and was a good performer though not a big name. There were six or seven acts on the bill, topped by singer Betty Miller. We got on well with Gerry, and he was good fun to work with. On the Thursday night the Scala Club was closed so we all went over to Scunthorpe to perform at a working men's club. The audience was nice but the backing left a lot to be desired. We all managed somehow, but Gerry had brilliant band parts, all beautifully arranged and written out. Well the organist and drummer just ruined his cat, as they couldn't read his music and missed key changes and changes of tempo. He came off in tears, got his gear together, climbed out of the dressing room window and drove away. A few years later we were booked to appear at the Coventry Theatre in variety, and top of the bill was – yes, you've guessed it – Engelbert Humperdinck. He'd just had a big hit with 'Release Me', and the theatre was packed. We went to his dressing room, and asked his manager if we could speak to Gerry. "Shush!" he said. "It's Engelbert now!" Anyway we went in, and he was very friendly and we recalled the old times. He hadn't changed – just his name. He was still the same old Gerry.

Brian:

In the late fifties we did our act on *The Vera Lynn Show* on ITV. She introduced us as "two very good friends of mine, The Patton Brothers", although we'd never met her before! We did a comedy routine to the 'Banana Boat Song' and a fast tap dance to 'Great Day'. Then Vera joined us and we did a song and dance to 'Sunny Side of the Street'. She had never danced before and we taught her this soft shoe routine which she soon picked up, and the audience loved it.

We had the pleasure of appearing with the great Johnny Ray (remember 'Cry'?) when he topped the bill at our local big club, the Greaseborough Social Club in Rotherham. It was magic to appear with such a big star from

Hollywood. He brought his own band but seemed to wear a very ordinary black dress suit, but he was brilliant.

Jimmy:

What I remember about Johnny Ray was that he wouldn't allow anybody on the side of the stage when he was on. I could understand that with a magician but not a singer!

Brian:

On that same bill were quite a few top club acts. Apart from us were Ronnie Dukes and Ricky Lee, Julian Jorg, Susan Maughan and many others. What they paid out that week I have no idea, but it packed the place all week! Great club, and great memories. The secretary/manager was Les Booth. He appeared on TV on the phone once, saying "'Ow much fer that Sammy Davis Junior?" – unfortunately he never did appear there. A great character was Les.

I first worked with Harry Secombe at Swansea, back in 1949, at a charity concert. I was with Billy West and His Harmony Boys, and the compere was Richard Attenborough! Later on, Jimmy and I appeared on his TV show in London. We entered bursting through a big paper circle in the studio, and went into 'Alabamy Bound', and a tap routine, and doing a spot. Then we did a lovely little comedy tap routine with Harry to

'Istanbul'. Jimmy played a monster in one part of the show, and Harry said, "That's Jimmy Patton there!" Harry was a lovely guy.

Jimmy:

Harry was very funny all the time and kept everyone roaring at rehearsals. He'd go to the loo singing 'Granada' at the top of his voice and blowing raspberries every few seconds. His wife Myra phoned straight after the live transmission to say how much she had enjoyed our routine.

The producer of that show was Bill Cotton Jr. We'd worked with his dad in the Billy Cotton Band Show at the Royalty Theatre, Chelsea. There was a great black dancer in the show called Ellis Jackson that we used to watch every night from the wings. Many years later we became very good friends with Gary Wilmot and we discovered that Ellis was his grandfather. So that's where some of Gary's terrific talent came from! Gary was in the revue show at Butlin's in Bognor Regis and we were the guest act every week. Even then you could see he was star material, doing excellent impersonations of all the stars.

We worked with Richard Hearne, better known as Mr Pastry, during the summer of 1967 at the Pavilion Theatre, Rhyl. I loved Rhyl after doing four seasons there at the Ampitheatre in the 50s, but it's more of a day-tripper's place, and business wasn't brilliant that summer. Though Richard had been a big star in the West End and on children's TV he was in the twilight of his career by then, but we certainly enjoyed working with him.

Brian:

We used to chat to him in his dressing room, and he even asked us to do another spot because his opening bit wasn't going down that well! He was explaining to the audience how he put his make up on, rather than doing his dancing routine as if a woman was there dancing with him, which didn't go down as he had hoped.

Jimmy:

We did a good sketch with him as three drunks going home after a night out. He'd had a very popular advert on television at the time, advertising Golden Wonder crisps, and every evening he'd give us several packets of crisps each! We loved them so much we never went hungry all season. When we worked at the Victoria Palace in 1981/2 Matthew Kelly came to see the show. He came backstage to say hello, and said, "You probably don't remember, but when you were playing at Rhyl with Mr Pastry, I was working backstage and my job was to mix up the paste for the custard pie routines!" He's certainly done well for himself since then!

During that Victoria Palace season we had the pleasure of working with two of the stars of *Dad's Army*: Arthur Lowe and Ian Lavender. It was *Mother Goose*: Arthur was the wicked squire and my brother and I were his rascally henchmen. Arthur suffered from an illness where he'd suddenly fall asleep – anytime, anywhere. He'd often be nodding off on the side of the stage and we'd have to nudge him and say, "Arthur! We're on!" We were told he was having supper with friends once, and his head suddenly dropped, eyes closed, straight into his soup. He was a nice man, though, and very generous: I remember him taking all the cast out for a meal at an Italian restaurant.

We became great pals with Ian. He lived with his girlfriend Mickey who was a choreographer, and she made us very welcome when we went to their house for dinner. We met up again in 1996 when we were both doing summer season in Eastbourne. He was at the Devonshire Park Theatre in *And Then There Were None* and *Out of Order.* We were at the Royal Hippodrome in *A Tribute to Al Jolson and the Minstrel Shows.* It was just like old times when we met up and we did several charity functions together. He's a great lad!

Brian:

We had the great pleasure of working with Billy Dainty in two pantomimes. The first was in 1959 at Cardiff, when he was Buttons in *Cinderella*, and the second one at Nottingham when he was playing Widow Twankey in *Aladdin*. I went round to see Billy at the Wakefield Theatre Club when he was with Rod Hull and Emu. The emu was in the corner but fortunately didn't get to attack me! Billy introduced me to Rod. saying: "Brian and Jimmy are the Patton Brothers, and they should be stars! They're a couple of great comics!" It was lovely of him to say so. Sadly, Billy took ill during the Nottingham pantomime and never appeared on stage again. A great loss to the business.

Jimmy Cricket was also in that show and we've got to know him very well over the years, though we only did the one pantomime with him, as well as one of his TV series. On his TV show we played four acrobats (me, Jimmy, the other Jimmy and Colin Bourdiec, a young guy who had done summer season with us at Berwick upon Tweed). It was a funny routine where none of us would do anything except shout "Ole" all the time! My wife Rachel and I and Jimmy and his wife Amy were recently invited to his birthday party in Manchester, which was a great night.

Jimmy:

Billy Dainty was Widow Twankey in our second panto together, as Brian said, and we were the Chinese policemen. We did an eccentric dance routine together which was great fun. Even at rehearsals Billy said that he'd strained his groin and it kept hurting. It got worse as the show went on and eventually he said, "Do you mind if we take the dance routine out, lads? I can't manage it any more." A few days later he was taken to Nottingham General Hospital, where they diagnosed cancer.

The other stars of the show, Jimmy Cricket and Barbara Windsor, got into a taxi with Brian and I between shows, and we went to visit Billy. He was always a practical joker, and a very funny man off stage as well as on. Even lying in his hospital bed he was cracking jokes and making everybody laugh. He told us how the day before, the nurse had told him the specialist had come to see him, and in walked Rod Hull in a white coat and stethoscope, who proceeded to make mayhem in the ward. He also said that a little boy had come into the hospital and said that he was a big fan and always watched him on television. He stayed for about half an hour, chatting about how funny Billy was and how much he made him laugh. Then as he was leaving he said, "And give my love to Schnorbitz!"

Only a few months later Billy passed away and the world of show business lost a great trouper. Sadly, Bernie Winters, the real owner of Schnorbitz, also died of cancer a few years after. Mike and Bernie were one of the most successful double-acts of the fifties and sixties, and they were smashing lads too. We met them in Australia in 1978 and saw them perform at the South Sydney Juniors Rugby League Club. It's a fabulous theatre bar and casino, very much like Las Vegas. We opened there the following week in *The Jolson Revue* and enjoyed a fabulous ten weeks in that wonderful country. (I'm very much a sun-worshipper so it was great to lie on Bondai Beach and Watson's Bay!) Mike and Bernie hadn't done their act for about six months, and we were sitting having a drink with them about half an hour before they were due on. They said, "We'd better have a quick talk-through to try to remember what we're going to do!" Of course it all came back as soon as they got on stage, and all their years of experience came into force. Real pros!

We've had great fun playing football for various showbiz teams. Most of the stars love sport which is good because, apart from the enjoyment, it helped a worthy cause. In 1959 it was Stan Stennet's Burkes Eleven against the TV All Stars. We had a huge crowd at the Leicester Speedway Stadium. Once the game was underway we all played it for real, especially Dave King, who was at that time one of the biggest stars on TV. He had all the gear, and rubbed on liniment just before we started. Of course, the result didn't matter on these occasions, but the atmosphere was electric. The same year I formed a team during the summer season, when I was in Jackson Earl's Melody Inn show. We played a big charity match against the *Army Game* team, who were appearing in Blackpool. Their captain was comedy actor Norman Rossington and they had a team of Italian jugglers playing for them – in spite of that (or perhaps because of it) we managed to win!

In Scarborough in 1965 I played in a charity cricket match and comedian Al Read was one of the big names. He loved cricket but he wouldn't come out. Once he was batting he just stayed there, even though he'd been bowled or caught out. We played a big game in Llandudno too, and in Colwyn Bay. That was for Alan Curtis's team, and Welsh comedian Wyn Colvin and Johnny Stewart were amongst the celebrities. I remember hitting a six there and it bounced just in front of the pavilion, hit the huge window, and bounced back without breaking the glass. That was a relief, I can tell you!

In 1977 we were in summer season in Babbacombe and we played in a charity cricket match against Tommy Steele's team, which included comedian Lennie Bennett, who got some big laughs by going around the ground carrying sandwiches in his cricketer's box which he took from his trousers, and offering them to the old ladies. The only thing that spoiled it for me happened during the tea break. We were all in the pavilion having a snack, and my kiddies Lee and Debbie asked Tommy Steele for his autograph. He said they had to go outside and queue with the rest of the public. We were all there giving our time for charity, and the least he could have done was to sign their books.

Another incident of someone not signing autographs happened at Weston Super Mare whilst I was appearing in summer show. It was a Sunday morning and I was in the park with my kids Lee and Debbie and my wife Val. Sitting a few yards away we noticed Frances de la Tour with her husband and children. Our kids loved her as Miss Jones in *Rising Damp*, as did we. They asked us if they could ask her for her autograph and we said yes, as long as they went up quietly and asked nicely, which they did. She didn't even look at them, and just said, "This is my day off. I don't give autographs on a Sunday." They were really disappointed, as you can imagine.

But most stars are nice, pleasant people. In the early fifties I was a big fan of the singer David Hughes. I saw him in lots of concerts, and was a member of his fan club. I've got all his records still! Here's an example of how nice a person he was. When Brian and I opened at the London Palladium in 1971 a telegram arrived on opening night that I still have. It read: YOU USED TO APPLAUD ME – NOW I APPLAUD YOU ON YOUR WELL-DESERVED SUCCESS – GOOD LUCK – DAVID HUGHES.

Now we'll tell you just how we came to appear at the Palladium – the ambition of all variety entertainers.

PLAYING THE PALLADIUM AND WORKING WITH RONNIE

Jimmy:

In January of 1962 TV producer Francis Essex phoned and said, "Would you do me a favour? Will you appear live on *Sunday Night at the Palladium*?" Would we? I should say so! He continued: "I can't tell you who it is yet as it's a secret, but a new compere is taking over from Bruce Forsyth. There's an Equity strike, so we can't use girl dancers. We'd like you to come on with the new compere and do a tap routine together." If there hadn't been an Equity strike we'd never have been asked to do it. We weren't in Equity then: we belonged to the Variety Artists Federation.

Brian:

We were thrilled, and knowing that the new host had to be someone who could tap dance said "Roy Castle?" "No," said Francis. "Norman Vaughan?" Francis said, "Got it in two! How did you guess that?" We said, "We thought of people who could tap dance, and who we'd worked with!" We'd worked with Norman at Blackpool's Queen's Theatre, and he came up to Birmingham where we were doing pantomime and rehearsed a tap routine to 'Varsity Drag'.

Jimmy:

Eventually the big night came – appearing on live television, at the greatest variety theatre in the world. What an atmosphere! We had cameras backstage, and as the show started they followed Norman going up the stage door-keeper and saying, "Which way is it to the stage?" He replied, "These two lads are just going on, go with them." Then the three of us strode from the back right down to the front of that fabulous stage. The lights blazed, the audience cheered, and we went straight into our fast tap routine to *Varsity Drag*. Francis Essex told us later that it was Val Parnell's idea. He said, "We'll either have Bruce Forsyth bring Norman on and say, 'this is what you do,' or we'll get the Patton Brothers to come on with him." Luckily the decision went our way!

Brian:

Half way through the routine Norman pretended to be puffed out, and said "Carry on lads" and leaned against the Proscenium Arch, tapping his chest. We finished the routine to big applause, and went off. Norman said "Who was that?" The audience never knew until the following week, when he said to them "The two guys dancing with me last week, were my pals The Patton Brothers.

Jimmy:

After we'd done our routine with Norman we were looking forward to the finale, and going around on the famous revolving stage with that famous signature tune. Unfortunately Tommy Steele overran with his act so the finale had to be cut at the last minute. Just my luck – but what a fabulous experience it was! The only thing that could top that would be to appear at the Palladium for a whole season, and less than ten years later we achieved that too.

Brian:

It was our greatest piece of luck, and it came in 1970. We were working with Ronnie Corbett at Birmingham's Alexandra Theatre. We didn't even know if Ronnie liked our act as his agent asked if we'd do our spot in a different place in the pantomime, as Ronnie was doing a piano bit straight afterwards. I did a bit from out front of house, when he said "Any requests?" I had to shout back "Walk Tall", which was a hit at the time, and Ronnie would say "Cheeky bugger!" which got a huge laugh. On the last night, he said he'd loved working with us, and hoped to work with us again. During our summer season at Clacton the following year we had a phone call from Ronnie saying "Have you fixed pantomime?" We said "Yes, unless it's the London Palladium!" He replied "It is!" We had to get out of our pantomime at Bradford, and they said they would release us if they could hire someone of our calibre for our money (which was very difficult!) They eventually got a club act, who wanted more money than we were on! So, in 1971 we were off to the London Palladium.

Jimmy:

After forty years in the business, Dad was really proud of us. It was something he'd never achieved. The pantomime was *Cinderella* and we were the Brokers Men, and what a thrill it was to appear on that stage!

97

The atmosphere was electric and at every performance there seemed to be someone famous in the audience. It was the longest running panto we ever appeared in – three weeks of rehearsals followed by a sixteen week run. It went on until after Easter! The only days off were Easter Monday and Good Friday. So what did Brian and I do? We worked both nights doing cabaret at Butlins, Bognor Regis!

Ronnie threw a big party at his house on the Easter Monday, but because of the cabaret Brian and I couldn't get there till after midnight! The party was still in full swing though, and it was great rubbing shoulders with the likes of Ronnie Barker, Jimmy Tarbuck and David Frost. Ronnie's wife Ann was a delightful hostess, and it was a pleasure to be invited.

Another time we were invited to Ronnie's house near Croydon for Sunday dinner and a film show. (That was before videos: Ronnie had an excellent film projector.) We had a lovely meal in pleasant company and finished up with a great movie: *Singin' in the Rain.* Brian dropped a verbal clanger. Cyd Charisse was doing a lovely dance routine, and Brian said: "I can't believe it, can you? There's Cyd Charisse, a beautiful, tall brunette, and she's going out with that little comic, Mickey Rooney. I wonder what she can see in him?" Then he suddenly realised what he said. After all, Ann is a tall lady and Ronnie was very short. So Brian tried to cover it up and said, "I mean, he's such a funny looking chap, isn't he!" The moment soon passed and was forgotten! It was my turn years later when Ronnie and Ann took Janet Brown, me my wife Val and Brian and his wife Rachel out for a meal in Bromley. It was a Chinese restaurant, and Val said, "I hope you've told Ronnie you don't eat Chinese food." I said, "I'll explain when we get there." I don't eat any foreign food – just plain English cooking. But when we arrived at the restaurant we realised Ronnie had ordered ahead, and all these exotic platters and dishes of Chinese food arrived! Val gave me a look and I had to blurt out that I don't eat anything like that. Ronnie was every understanding, and called the waiter over so I could explain to him. All's well that ended well – and the French fries were delicious!

Ronnie proved to be a great friend to us through the years, and we ended up doing nine pantomimes together. He also used us on a lot of his TV variety shows. Ann is lovely too, and we worked with her (as Ann Hart) on Sunday concerts at Butlin's while she was at the Victoria Palace with the Crazy Gang. Since then, their daughter Sophie has done four shows with us, starting as a prop girl, then a dancer, then Dandini, and then Jill in *Mother Goose.* She started at the bottom and worked her way up – a real pro like her parents.

Brian:

The cast in that first Palladium panto read like a who's who of show business at that time: Ronnie, Clodagh Rogers, Terry Scott, David Kossoff, Julian Orchard, Malcolm Roberts and of course the Patton Brothers. Julian was great, because he was a 'gangling' sister against Terry Scott's 'chunky' sister! He was a lovely guy and sent us a good luck telegram the following year at Bristol in the same pantomime. We loved Julian. Clodagh was wonderful too, as was Malcolm. One day he had Jack Jones as a guest in his room, who at that time was going out with the lovely Susan George who came to visit us in our dressing room to chat. She had just starred in *Straw Dogs* with Dustin Hoffman, and said that Dustin, being a method actor, had suddenly slapped her face before a big scene, because she was supposed to hate him. That's some method acting!

We loved them all, although we didn't get close to Terry Scott, who played one of the ugly sisters. He was a very funny comedian but very different offstage. (Some comedians are like that, while others are always trying to be funny.) I held the door open for him one day, and he didn't even say thank you. He would wear a long black kaftan at the break of the shows, and he would have some of the girl dancers in his dressing room reading their palms! We didn't get to know him very well, although he did enjoy the football sweep that Jimmy ran every Saturday. (His team was Watford, and he followed them fervently.)

Terry had played an ugly sister at the Palladium before. One day he was in Ronnie Corbett's dressing room when Danny La Rue popped in. Terry asked him what he thought of it, and Danny said, "Excellent!" Terry replied, "But we haven't got a star like Cliff Richard playing Buttons!" Ronnie said, "Cheeky bugger!" and rightly so! At rehearsal the director (Albert Knight, a lovely man) said, "The splosh routine that Terry and Julian are doing has to be cut!" Terry Scott said, "What's Corbett taking out?" To which he was told: "Nothing to do with you!"

David Kossoff played the Baron. He was a lovely fella and a real gentleman. He said to us, "You two are teaching me the lot about pantomime," which was lovely for him to say considering the work he had done. He did a lovely routine "I'm shy Mary Ellen, I'm shy", which he did again and again at rehearsals, but unfortunately the pantomime was running over and so the song was cut!

In his autobiography, Ronnie wrote: "The Patton Brothers are a wonderfully funny double-act. Every time I have done a pantomime I have tried to get the Patton Brothers in it as well." He was a great friend, and we still miss him very much.

Jimmy:

Brian and I were staying in digs in Golders Green with a pal of ours, comedian Charlie Stewart. David lived nearby, and he learned that we used to travel in by tube every day. "Listen, boys," he said, "I usually drive here in a Mini, but some days I come in the Daimler. On those nights I'll give you a lift home." That he did, and we travelled like lords on those occasions!

The reason we travelled in on the underground was that we both had car trouble. The lock had gone on the nearside door of Brian's and it was tied up with rope inside! As for me, after the first four weeks of the run my car was stolen. I used to leave it by Regent's Park, and one night after the show I just kept walking, and wondering if I'd left it further away... I ended up in Camden Town before I realised it had been stolen. (Luckily I got it back ten days later!)

One day Ronnie came up to us and said he had some good news for us. He told us that scriptwriter Bryan Blackburn was arranging a new Saturday night variety show for ITV and he wanted a new Saturday night variety show for ITV and he wanted Brian and me to compere the show each week. We were over the moon. We'd done lots of TV appearances but only as guests on other people's shows. What you need to make a name is to be seen regularly on TV. The powers that be said that as we were appearing nightly at the Palladium we could record the show on a Sunday night. That was perfect for us! We waited anxiously for further details and then came the bad news. They decided to do it live on a Saturday night, so obviously we were no longer available. That kind of opportunity has never come our way since. Instead, a then-unknown comedian called Larry Grayson got the job and grabbed the chance with both hands! Oh well – that could have been us.

The last night party on stage at the Palladium was wonderful. The entire cast and the crew were there with guests and it was very enjoyable. I was with my wife Val and Brian was with his first wife Christine. There were some lovely engraved ashtrays dotted about the tables which had 'London Palladium 1971/72' on them. We all wanted one as a souvenir but didn't like to take them. Later on Clodagh Rogers, who made a wonderful Cinderella, came up to us, opened up her handbag, and popped one in! After that we all followed suit and so well have lovely mementoes to look back on. Val, Brian and Christine were all merry on brandy, and though I don't drink at all I couldn't have been in a happier frame of mind.

Brian:

We have so many wonderful memories of that pantomime. We got a great write-up in *The Stage* saying, ""When they are big stars at a Royal Command performance, they'll remember this!" which was lovely to hear. There were real ponies in the show, galloping on a treadmill. The Duchess of Kent was in the royal box with her children for one performance, and other celebrity visitors included Jimmy Edwards, Mike and Bernie Winters, Larry Grayson, Pauline Collins and John Alderton, Peter Osgood... the list goes on! Peggy Mount came backstage and said "I wish I could tap dance" in that fabulous deep voice of hers. Lovely Ronnie Barker came too, but he had lost his voice, so just had to write things down! We met him again later, and we asked him if he had ever done pantomime. His answer was no, he had never done one - such a shame, we thought.

Tony Blackburn said lovely things about us on his radio shows, and so did Pete Murray. He came to see his friend Malcolm Roberts, but although we weren't names he took the time to knock on our door and said, "I couldn't pass your door, lads, without saying how much I enjoyed your performance." It meant so much to us, and the next day on his radio show he say that the Patton Brothers were the best Brokers Men he'd ever seen. Danny La Rue told us he wanted us the following year at Manchester. But Ronnie wanted us with him, and said we'd have a lot more to do, so we stayed with Ronnie and joined him the following year at the Bristol Hippodrome.

Jimmy and I weren't happy for a while because Ronnie had told us that we would have a lot more to do but Dick Hurran, when we did dress rehearsal, said, "I only want what you did at the Palladium." We stormed off stage because of Ronnie's promise, and Ronnie came to pacify us. "What's up lads?" he asked us. We told him, and Ronnie promised to have a word with Hurran. We were then given more to do, and were appeased.

Clodagh Rogers was back for this season too, and we were joined by John Inman and Barry Humphries as the ugly sisters. We had to share the dressing room with our pal Charlie Stewart and his dog 'Chuffer'. The dog would sit in the doorway. We would step over it to go in or out, we liked the window closed, and when we came back to our room it was open. He turned our telly off, and we'd put it back on again, so it wasn't ideal! Charlie was playing Cinderella's father, Baron Hardup. He did a gag during the show about Cinders which Clodagh didn't like. Charlie said that he had to smack her bottom one day, and she looked in the mirror at her bottom and said tearfully, "Oh you've cracked it!" She complained, and the gag was cut!

Tony Adams (of *Crossroads* fame) was the Prince. One day he came for a meal at the next door café with us and said "I won't be coming here again" – it wasn't up to his standards! He was a lovely guy though. Jimmy had a bad back. Tony massaged it and said "You've got a very young back!" For this season we also had an extremely famous visitor – Bristol boy Cary Grant came with his mother, who was in her nineties at the time!

In 1973 the show went to the Manchester Palace with the same cast, apart from Tony Adams who was replaced by Brian Hills. We got our dressing room sorted this year so we could be on our own! It was another very good season. John and Barry did a very funny gag at a party. They dressed as two nuns, and did some very funny chat, turned and walked away, and had no backs to their outfits, just bare bottoms. It got a huge laugh from everyone assembled! We went to see Harry Secombe at the Golden Garter, a huge club. We chatted backstage and he told us that he did more singing then, and not so much comedy as he was doing *Songs of Praise* by then. He was great, though: just the same as ever.

So we'd had three great years with Ronnie. Over the years we also did many more panto performances with him, and appeared in his television series. Ronnie's family often came to see us, and eventually Ronnie's daughter Sophie did pantomime with us. I was in the garden when Rachel told me Ronnie had died, and I burst into tears. He was such a great person in our life. He even came down to my eightieth birthday party with his lovely wife Anne, and I shall never forget the privilege of having him there. Dear Ronnie.

THE SHOW MUST GO ON!

Jimmy:

In this business, you have to be able to improvise. Back in 1952 I was playing Simple Simon in *Babes in the Wood* at the Grand Theatre, Llandudno, and the following week we went to the Theatre Royal, Bilston. When we arrived there on the Sunday, we discovered they'd already done a production of *Babes in the Wood* the week before. So the boss said, "Never mind – we'll do *Red Riding Hood*!" One day's rehearsal and we did it! All the three-handed gags and front cloth routines stayed, and Maid Marion became Red Riding Hood! It was all very hectic and panicky but everything went well and the audience never realised we'd had to change it all so quickly. Everything's okay so long as the audience enjoy the show and go out happy. Our job is to make it all seem as seamless as possible. But behind the scenes, it's not always plain sailing!

I remember one time when we played the Cabaret Club in Liverpool, and it was quite an eventful week! It was a plush cabaret room with a glass stage in small squares. We had just finished our 'Istanbul' routine with a comedy step – and crash! One of the glass squares shattered and fell through, leaving a gaping hole in the stage. It got a roar from the audience and we just carried on with the act as though nothing had happened. The same week, the compere said: "Ladies and gentlemen – The Patton Brothers!" And with that, every light in the club went out. There was nothing – no lights anywhere; no music; not a sound. Nobody knew what to do. Eventually for security reasons the manager asked everyone to leave the club. So we had a night off, which we didn't mind at all!

Things often go wrong on first nights, and it was no exception at the Prince's Theatre, Torquay when Brian and I walked on from the back of the stage as the orchestra played the intro to our first number. As we were halfway down, a cloth was supposed to drop down behind us, and we'd go into our song. It worked like a charm at rehearsal, but on the night the cloth came down too soon – right in front of us. Bang! We were stuck behind the curtains, which had no centre opening. By the time we'd dashed to the side of the stage and came to the front our song was halfway through. So I just started leaping about, doing eccentric dance steps and slapping Brian's face, and I don't think the audience even realised what had gone wrong.

When your audience is made up of fellow professionals, however, it's harder to hide the problems! Jimmy Cricket is a pal and a smashing lad. He's always got a smile and a joke for everyone. We've worked in pantomime and old time music hall together, and appeared as guests on his TV show *And There's More.* It was after we'd appeared on that show that the producer rang us up and said that after the last show in the series they were having a party for Jimmy, and would we like to do the cabaret? So everything was agreed and nobody told Jimmy. We told the producer that we need good backing for our musical numbers, and two microphones and plenty of room for our tap dancing routine.

On the big night we went to the Central TV studios in Nottingham and watched the recording of the show but were kept hidden from Jimmy. The party was in a nightclub in the city centre, so we made our way there and couldn't believe what we found! As we walked in, we asked where the stage was. In the corner of the room was a tiny platform, about seven feet wide and shaped like a triangle. Remember, there was supposed to be two of us doing a comedy routine on there! We told them we'd finish the act with a fast tap routine and guess what, the stage was carpeted. We asked for the two microphones and were given one, with an impossibly short lead. So we asked where the pianist was, and the DJ said, "I can play a bit." We couldn't believe it! We gave the lad our music and he said he couldn't read it and played by ear! By now we were really beginning to panic! They were all due in the club in about half an hour – Jimmy, Joan Sims, Nicholas Smith, writer Eddie Braben and producer Jon Schofield among them. Obviously we couldn't tap dance on carpet, so we got a long table top from the back of the club and laid it on the stage. (So far so good!) We set the microphone at the front but the lead came up in the air to the plug which was halfway up the wall, which meant we'd have to do our patter standing at either side of the wire. As for music, the DJ didn't know any of the tunes that we wanted to do. We said we opened with 'Cabaret' – he couldn't play that, so we said, "just give us 'vamp' and keep going!" For the tap routine we wanted 'Bye Bye Blues' but he'd never heard of it, so we said just play anything fast. At that moment we were told Jimmy was on his way, so we dashed into our dressing room. Except, it wasn't a dressing room. We got changed in the kitchen, among the plates and the cooker.

Once everyone was settled into their seats we were introduced as 'a big surprise for Jimmy'. We got a great reception, so that made us feel good, at least! What he played on the piano for our opener I have no idea, but somehow we sang 'Cabaret' to it. I do some eccentric knockabout after that, but on a stage that size with a microphone with trailing lead it was difficult, to say the least. We grabbed a chair from the audience and did our *Mastermind* routine which went great. Time for the big finish! We had to throw the mic stand out of the way, make sure the table top was steady on the carpeted stage, and do the tap routine huddled together on the tiny stage. For the finale we throw ourselves on the floor and kick our legs out horizontally for half a chorus. We did our fast tap and then shouted, "one, two, three, four, five, six, seven, eight!" but the pianist just sat there grinning at us. (He told us later he'd been laughing at the gags so much he'd forgotten he was supposed to be playing for us.) We shouted again and he played something we'd never heard of, and quite possibly he hadn't either. But at least it was fast! We finished with a big leap in the air and then down on our knees. The pianist had his head down and didn't realise, so he just kept on playing like the clappers. The audience realised the difficulties we'd been working under and gave us a marvellous reception which made everything worthwhile. We all had a lovely meal and it ended up being a great party... but I'd never want to go through anything like that again!

There's nothing worse than going to see a show only to find the star isn't appearing. It's such a disappointment. We did nine pantomimes with Ronnie Corbett and he never missed a performance in all those years. I was Ronnie's understudy in Birmingham in 1969/70 and even with a bad dose of flu he still went on for the matinee. The same can be said for John Inman, who we did six pantomimes with, even when he spent a night in hospital in Oxford at Christmas with kidney stones. Most of the stars have that attitude, and don't want to let the public down. Sometimes it can be touch and go, though!

Back in 1958 we were in pantomime at the Palace Theatre, Leicester. One afternoon, six of us from the show decided to go over to Nottingham to see their matinee. I had a new Ford Consul which could easily seat six, and it was only about 25 miles away, so we had plenty of time to get back for the evening performance. We were enjoying the panto until at about 4.30 the theatre manager came and told us that a very thick fog had descended and that perhaps we ought to set off back. Well, I've never seen fog like it

– a real pea-souper. The traffic was at a standstill, barely crawling along, bumper to bumper. After an hour we had scarcely moved and were starting to panic. Johnny Harris, who was our company stage manager, got out a t a phone box and had time to call the theatre and tell them to put the understudies on. We eventually got to the theatre at about 8.30, when the interval was on. Brian and I were okay because we did our act in the second half, but that's the nearest I've ever come to missing a show.

When we were doing the revue *Honky Tonk* in 1955 I had the flu. I'd taken Beecham's powders and my bed was soaking wet with sweat. I felt weak and drained so I sent for the theatre doctor. He gave me an injection just before the curtain went up and I went on okay. No one ever dreamed of missing a performance in those days. The same thing happened when I was playing the good robber in panto at the Theatre Royal, Exeter: the theatre doctor gave me an injection before the show and on I went. During the fight scene with Brian I could tell I was going to be sick. I dashed off stage, was sick in the fire bucket, dashed back on and carried on with the fight scene as if nothing had happened. The same illness hit me again at the Gaiety Theatre, Dublin, and every scene I'd just lay on the floor of the dressing room until it was time to go on again. It's amazing really, but no matter how bad you feel, once you're in front of the audience you do your stuff. In a pantomime at the Alexandra, Birmingham, I had a terrible cold and laryngitis. It was twice daily and I just kept going, even though I sounded like Francis the Talking Mule.

At the Amphitheatre, Rhyl in 1957, Brian was rushed into hospital with acute appendicitis. I did a single act instead of our double act while he recovered but he was soon back on his feet and back in the show, doing everything apart from the dancing routines. Then at the Bristol Hippodrome [WHAT YEAR?] I was in the digs one morning and bent down to open a drawer when something snapped in my back. I was in agony and couldn't straighten up. We had a matinee to do that afternoon and I just couldn't see how I could do it. I walked to the theatre like Richard the Third. Once I was there I collapsed on the settee in the dressing room, and when it was time for the show someone had to get hold of me and pull me up. But as the orchestra played our entrance music, Brian and I leapt on stage with an eccentric dance routine that ended with me doing a fall flat out. As soon as I came off the pain returned and I couldn't straighten up again. But every time I went back on stage I did everything fine, including the fast tap routine and the acrobatic act with Ronnie Corbett.

In pantomimes there's lots of glitter and gold dust sprinkled everywhere, and one Christmas another thing happened to me. One Saturday during the matinee I got something in my eye and it was very irritating. I drove home to Rotherham at the weekend and kept trying to clear my eye with eyewash but nothing would clear it. Every time I blinked it was awful. After the matinee on Monday I drove up to the Stockport Eye Hospital, and they were brilliant. They put my head in a clamp so I couldn't move and then the doctor sprayed some liquid in my eye, which took away any feeling. Then he got some tiny tweezers and pulled out a piece of gold metal which was lodged firmly in my pupil. I didn't feel a thing and it was such a relief. I'd had to drive there with one eye closed, and had done a couple of shows in the same condition. You don't appreciate your health until something's wrong.

In the summer of 1965 we were in the show *Dazzle* at the Spa Theatre, Scarborough. While we were there a group of us entertainers played a charity football match against their local team. A big crowd was at the ground, and everything was going great until just before half time, when I streaked past a defender and he whipped my legs from under me. I tried to carry on but I could hardly walk, and had to make my way to the dressing room. When I got to the theatre I was limping badly and had my ankle strapped up. I managed to do all the sketches and gags but there was no way that I could do our tap dancing. The next morning my ankle was black and blue so I went straight to the doctor and he sent me to the hospital for an x-ray. It was broken, so I had a plaster put on right the way up to my knee. They said, "You can't do the show tonight as the plaster won't be dry." There was no way I was going to miss the show, so I sat on the sun terrace at my digs in the sun with the electric fire on a long lead, and stayed there all afternoon until the plaster was dry. And so for the last six weeks of the summer season I did the show hobbling about on stage, with my left leg encased in plaster!

It was quite an eventful year, 1965. There was the wonderful thrill of my son Lee being born... and the less wonderful experience of having my ankle broken! Worse was to come, though. In October I was driving down to Sutton Coldfield to do a week's cabaret at La Reserve Restaurant. It was early morning and there was thick fog everywhere. You could only see about 25 yards in front of you. I stopped in a line of traffic behind a lorry waiting to move off. Suddenly I heard the sound of another lorry screaming up behind me. I looked in the mirror, but all I could see was thick fog. Then I heard the sudden squealing of brakes, and all hell broke loose. I was thrown about all over the car, hitting my head on the windscreen. It seemed to go on forever and the noise was deafening. Then suddenly everything was peaceful and calm. I thought I was in heaven. My car was smashed between the two lorries, and was just a mangled wreck. I was lying on the floor in the front of the car where the passenger seat was. If there had been seatbelts in those days I would never have survived. I'd have been crushed in my seat. Someone came over to the wreck and I moved my hand. I heard someone say, "He's alive! Is there anyone else in the car?" They managed to get me out somehow, and carried me to the side of the road, where a policeman covered me with his cape. I was in a daze but all I was worried about was the car and what was going to happen to it. I remember a woman asking me if I wanted a cup of tea, then looking at me and saying, "Oh, it's his ear isn't it?" I'd hit the windscreen with the side of my head. The ambulance arrived, and I passed out. When I came round I was en route to Chesterfield General Hospital. I had dozens of stitches in my ear, head and finger, but luckily my face wasn't cut. X-rays revealed I had also fractured several vertebrae in my back. I had palpitations and dizzy spells for weeks afterwards. I had always had perfect eyesight, but from that point on I've had to wear glasses.

Brian had already got to the venue and was told about the accident then. He phoned me at the hospital and remembers the nurse saying, "Turn his head so that he can hear." It was lucky he had phoned me, because on his way to the hospital he passed the scene of the crash and spoke to the policeman, who told him the driver of the car was dead. It was a long time ago now but I can remember every detail vividly. They put a photograph of my smashed car on the front page of the *Sheffield Star and Telegraph.* The headline was: 'Alive After This!'

PANTOMANIA!

Brian:

Our first pantomime as a double act was at Wimbledon Theatre in "Aladdin" where we were playing "Chinese Policemen". The Director, Peter Haddon, introduced everyone on the first day, and said: "These two lads, are the Patton Brothers, and they are going to fall down and make the kiddies laugh." (What an introduction!) We had a great season, and we had the Peter Haddon players in most roles, but Douglas Byng was top of the bill and Jasmine Dee was second top. The only other variety act was Jimmy and I.

Duggie Byng was a good comedian, but afflicted by a very bad nervous twitch in his neck and face when he was offstage. On stage he could usually control it, then as soon as he came off it would start again. But there was one time when we were doing a courtroom scene, with me and Jimmy dressed as two policemen either side of him, when he suddenly did a massive twitch fully the equal of Jack Douglas. The audience thought it was all part of the show! Jasmine Dee was a very good principal boy as well. But the old actor playing the Emperor, Hugh Dempster, knew nothing about the script, as he had just got back from playing in a role in Broadway, and had failed to learn it!

The following year we were at Glasgow Pavilion with the great Scottish comic Jack Milroy and Robert Wilson with the White Heather Group. Also in the cast was an act called the Four Ramblers, one of whom penned some band parts. You may remember his name – it was the great Val Doonican! We met him again after he rocketed to fame and he was still the same charming man. When we were doing panto at the Gaiety Theatre in Dublin, Val came on the Sunday to do *Live at the Gaiety* on TV, and he used our dressing room. When we arrived the following day there was a lovely letter from Val thanking us and reminiscing about the old days.

Robert Wilson was a star singer. When Goldilocks got into bed, the back door would fling open and in came Robert and the White Heather group, and performed a twenty minute spot, very loudly. Then they went out the door, in came the three bears, and the pantomime continued! It was all such fun. Juel Morrell (Eddie Morrell's daughter) was principal girl. A lovely girl with a nice singing voice and lovely personality, she had been in summer season at Morecambe for her dad, the same season that I had been with Billy West and his Harmony Boys.

Our third pantomime was at Leicester Palace. Anna Dawson was Cinderella, a lovely lass who later married John Boulter from the Black and White Minstrel shows. Freddie Sales was top of the bill, and he was well known for doing a spot as a baby in a cot. He'd bang on the side of the cot with a spoon, and say with a baby's voice: "Go bang with the 'poon!" A very funny bit – he wore a huge nappy! He went to Las Vegas later on in his career and did well, I believe.

Jimmy and I weren't married men back then, so Jimmy took out Anna Dawson, and I took out one of the dancers. One day we all went to see Jewel and Warriss at the Coventry Theatre, and during the interval the manager came over and said, "The fog is very thick out there, and you ought to set off back now!" We went outside to find ourselves in the middle of a real pea souper! The car was full as we had Cinders, Dandini, the Brokers men (that was us) - plus the company manager! We phoned in from a call box (no mobiles in those days), and said we'd not get there in time for the curtain up. They put Cinders and Dandini's understudies on for the start of the show (both girls were in tears in the car) but they let Jim and I do our spot when we arrived. We even played the comedy horse!

In 1959 we played the New Theatre, Cardiff. It was the same pantomime, but a different top of the bill: Billy Dainty and the Welsh comedian Ossie Morris. Billy was great and a lovely guy, but his wife wouldn't let him play in a charity football match. He did great eccentric dancing, and his wife was concerned about the danger to his legs! Ossie suffered terribly with piles, and had a TV in his dressing room to watch the Welsh rugby games (on a comfortable cushion)!

In 1960 we went to the Theatre Royal, Exeter, where we were in *Babes in the Wood* with Anne Daly, Danny O'Dea and Jean Barrington (who later married Duggie Chapman). An old actor, who had been at the theatre in pantomime for years, would leap through the curtains at the start and in a deep voice would shout, "Behold!" which frightened all the children sitting in the audience. One act that he announced over the microphone was: "Miss Darly and her dogs, and her amazing chimpanzees!" One chimp grabbed my then girlfriend (and future wife) and threw her on the floor. She screamed and turned red with embarrassment and fright, and the chimp was pulled off her!

Danny O'Dea was a good Dame, but when he got heckled by some young lads in the box, he took off his wig at the interval and said he'd sort them out! They stopped heckling and shouting after that! We shared a dressing room with the baddie, Charles Gillespie. One night after a meal where baked beans figured prominently on the menu, my body let out a small explosion. Charles was a bit upset, and in a posh voice said "That's not on, Brian!" (Needless to say we all tittered for the rest of the show that day!)

In 1961 we went to the Alexandra Theatre in Birmingham to play in *Aladdin* once again. The cast included Ted Hockridge (a great singer from West End musicals), Joe Church (a very good comic), Miki and Griff, Terry Fearis, Tommy Rose and Jimmy and I. Miki and Griff got their big hit *A Little Bitty Tear* just before the pantomime, so they were lifted above Joe for the show later. They were lovely people, though Miki would play ten pin bowling all morning and occasionally drop down in a faint after the finale! (The stage hands would have to dash to help her up.) They said that if their record would go to number one or two, they would throw a party. It only reached number 16... but they were lovely people!

The producer/director Derek Salberg was a peculiar guy. He would throw a party every Saturday night and would walk up to you and say hello and then walk away! He never stayed and chatted for any length of time like people normally do. He came into our dressing room the year after, and said to Jimmy as he was wet shaving: "That's almost archaic, Jimmy!" (Jimmy still wet shaves to this day!)

We did a charity show at the theatre with Lonnie Donegan topping the bill. Also on the bill was Ted Rogers, Mike and Bernie Winters and Joe Church. Mike and Bernie and Jimmy and I finished our act with a tap routine and at the end of the first half some idiots put a carpet down on the stage. Jimmy and I can improvise our way around most obstacles, but tap dancing on a carpet just can't be done! So they took it up in the second half so that we could all dance.

In 1963 we went to the Princess Theatre, Torquay with the same pantomime, but an almost completely different cast. Top of the bill was South African singing star Eve Boswell, who was very good. Miki and Griff were there again too. We did lots of bowling with Micki (but not Griff), and I remember she loaned me her Mini Minor car when my car went in to be mended. I was now married to my first wife, Christine, who was a dancer in the pantomime. We went to a fancy dress ball one night, and I wore one of the curtains from the digs! When we got back we couldn't get in, as the door was locked, so Christine and I had to ring the bell. I had to hide the curtains under my mac so that the landlady didn't notice!

This was the first pantomime that we met and performed with Bobby Dennis, who like me had been a Billy West Harmony Boy, although before I had joined the group. Bobby and Jimmy and I had some great times filled with much laughter. Jimmy was sitting in the cinema when a voice shouted out "Jimmy, Jimmy Patton!" It was Bobby – the first time they met! He was asking us for any good sketches he could perform as he was going out to Australia for the first time. He became well known out there. A lovely, nutty guy Bobby is still with us in his nineties and we're still great friends.

It was back to Wolverhampton in 1964 – John Hanson, Arthur Worsley, Tommy Fields (Gracie's brother), Billy Burden and us. Arthur was a lovely guy and the greatest ventriloquist of his time. You could see his wonderful vent doll sat in an upstairs window of his house in South shore, Blackpool. He and his wife Audrey came to see my lovely baby daughter, Julie, at

Fleetwood. John was a great singer from musicals, but would belt out the songs at rehearsals and then loudly cough up phlegm on stage, spitting it out only when the action was on the other side of the stage! He was a stickler for making things look real. He did a fight scene with the Sheriff of Nottingham and his sword came down so powerfully that it landed right on top of Anthony Benson's bald head! The blood spurted up into the air but somehow Anthony kept going to the end of the scene. It was almost the end of the show so they whipped him off to hospital for a couple of stitches and he was fine the next day.

Billy was a good comic who liked very large girls! We were at a cricket match and we heard him say, "Look at that!" We looked, expecting a beautiful girl, but this rather rotund lady was walking by!

In 1966 we were at the Sheffield Lyceum for *Cinderella*. We were the Broker's Men, Dickie Valentine was top of the bill as Buttons, and Cardew Robinson and Joe Black played the ugly sisters. Dickie was excellent but we only had one central microphone and he asked if he minded it being turned up for him. We didn't mind, because we could be heard alright! It was a very enjoyable run and Jimmy got his first house built during it (and he's still in it to this day!) It was built by our sister's then husband, Pete. Pamela Gale was an excellent Prince. Pamela has a lovely soprano voice, and Wendy, as Cinders, had a deep, soubrette type of voice. It seemed funny when the Prince sang love songs in this beautiful high voice, and Cinderella was singing 'Give Me the Simple Life' in this low, raunchy voice.

1968 took us to the City Varieties in Leeds for *Cinderella*. We'd done summer season for Terry Cantor with his son, Kenny, and he asked us to go to Leeds with Kenny. It was the first time that the City Varieties had put on a pantomime after years without one. We rehearsed the dress rehearsal up to the interval and then as the time was getting late, Terry said, "It'll go on alright, see you in the morning!" So we went to see our team Rotherham United play a cup match at Mansfield. We lost, and I pranged the car getting there! Not my fault though!

We did a pilot with Kenny for Yorkshire TV which hadn't started yet, but unfortunately it was never shown. It was called *Cantor's Crackers*, with Kenny, us and Jane Terry. The pantomime had a good pro cast, though dressing room wise, it was Kenny and the Dame (Ken Barnes, a lovely guy and comic) in Number One, then the uglies (Grande and Mars) in Number Two, and Wendy King (Dandini), Barbara Jackson (principal boy) and Linzi Jane (Cinderella) in Number Three. Then upstairs in one room – us, John Warwick (Barbara's husband) and all the rest of the male cast. Great guys but too many for one room!

In 1974 we were in Birmingham for *Babes in the Wood*. Leslie Crowther was top of the bill, and also in the cast was Arthur Tolcher – remember "Not now, Arthur!" on *The Morecambe and Wise Show*? He told us, "It's amazing becoming a star at my time of life." We were in our favourite parts – the robbers – which we loved playing. Jimmy was the good robber and I was the bad robber. We performed comedy boxing, fencing and shooting to music. We had to lock away the guns after each show. I'd shoot Jimmy's trousers off, and he'd do the same to me! A stage hand at each side would pull the back of our velcroed trick trousers as the bang of the gun was heard and they would fly off into the wings. One time as

Jimmy fired I realised I hadn't got my trick trousers on, they just ripped and hung there! It got a great laugh though!

We did the same show the following year at the Theatre Royal, Nottingham, then again the year after at the Pavilion Theatre, Bournemouth. But because Bournemouth had a different version of the same show the year before, we retitled it *Robin Hood*! But once again, it was a great pantomime. We even had a picture of us as the robbers pretending to steal an old Rolls Royce left out at the front of the theatre. It had been wonderful working with Leslie and Jack for three years on the trot.

In 1977 we were with Bill Maynard in *Jack and the Beanstalk* in Norwich. Bill was a great guy who was funny offstage as well as on. George Lacey was one of the best Dames in the business. Bill said that George had said to him, "These lads are doing a lot in it, aren't they?" Bill replied, "Yeah, but it's all good stuff, isn't it?"

We went all the way up to Scotland for our next pantomime, over the bridge from Edinburgh into Fife for *Babes in the Wood*. We were sharing top of the bill with Russell Hunter whose main claim to fame was playing 'Lonely' in *Callan* with Edward Woodward. He was a lovely guy and we did quite a lot of business with him in the pantomime. In the pantomime story we were the two Robbers who had to take two youngsters into the woods - they were almost our size! We had the Wychwoods on the bill too – this was a famous dog act, but by now the daughter of the originals, with her husband. They were given a room for the dogs, which was almost a 'no go area' and not from fear of being bitten! The smell was quite something.

For 1979 we played in *Mother Goose* in Oxford. Our old friend John Inman was now the top star, having hit it big in *Are You Being Served?* Another old friend, Billy Burden joined us on the bill. He was a lovely guy, but didn't suffer fools, and was a jealous man. His girlfriend, Suzie, was a large but pretty lady, and he got jealous and said he'd "hammer" some guys in the bar next to the theatre, who he thought were chatting her up. However he relented, and nothing came of it. We did the same show again the next year, this time in Stockport. It was great to work with John again, and this time we were second top, as Billy Burden didn't do the show. But the billing in the programme didn't have Jimmy and me in the 'number two' position which we were most upset with. I went to the young guy who had been in charge of the programme and asked why? He said – he had copied the position of the previous cast line up and didn't realise there was a "pecking order"!!! (By the way the last years' double comics had been "Harman and Elliott" (Barry and Paul, our brothers!!) who weren't a "name" back then of course! He said that they would change the programme once they had sold the printed copies in their store. I asked him how many there were!! He told me about 30,000!!!! Needless to say, the change didn't occur!

Eddie Large of Little and Large came backstage and chatted with us: a lovely guy. He said that he and Syd had seen us at the Palladium with Ronnie Corbett and really liked the act. All the time we were talking my uncle Len insisted on playing a tape recording of his prowess on a Hammond organ – which was excruciating! The more we talked to Eddie, the louder Uncle Len turned up the machine! Family eh?

And it was *Mother Goose* with John once again in 1981, though this time we were at London's Victoria Palace. We were honoured once again to go back into the West End. (It would have been the London Palladium but they weren't doing pantomime, so the Victoria Palace took over.) This time we were joined by *Dad's Army*'s Arthur Lowe and Ian Lavender, and Arthur, Jimmy and I had a lovely song spot together. They were great guys and performers and we got on so well with them all. Arthur and his wife Joan threw a lovely party meal for Rachel on her birthday in January, and gave her a fabulous book on all the stories of the ballets, which they both signed, and she still owns. Barbara Newman played the goose again, and in the finale one night she fell over as the curtain was closed and caught her goose head, knocking her over in front of the main tabs! She lay there until she was rescued with her legs in the air! She went to a cast party at John's lovely flat, and had trodden in something which she walked up the stairs and into his lounge!! Oh dear, oh dear, what a mess!

We were hoping that the season would be extended as had been promised due to the wonderful business we were doing, but Elizabeth Taylor was booked to follow us into the theatre in *The Little Foxes*, and they needed time to accommodate her requirements. She had insisted that one wall of her dressing room should be turned into an aquarium so that she could watch the fish swimming around to relax. Also, the route from her dressing room

right to the side of the stage had to be carpeted in white piled carpet. So we had to finish two weeks earlier than we should have done.

Not every pantomime was a great experience, so I suppose for the sake of variety I should include one we didn't enjoy too much. This was *Aladdin* at the Theatre Royal, Nottingham, in 1985. First of all, we were shoved upstairs while a very nasty guy who was company manager had a downstairs room. I also hated the big time director, who Charlie Stewart had told us only ever went to visit the 'stars' in No. 1 and No. 2 dressing room. Jimmy and I were relegated to the first room upstairs. We were down to do a spot and when we said we did a longer spot normally, as we got to the side of the stage to do the act, this prat of a stage manager guy said "It's out!" The cast were lovely, but we didn't over enjoy the pantomime. We did however enjoy the ice cream gag that we did with Jimmy Cricket, and Billy Dainty got us to do a comedy bit with him. This too was a let-down, because as we went to rehearse (after not being told anything about it) we found out from Billy we were the comedy horse! He said, "I'll tell the audience it's you!" We'd gone especially to rehearse in London, too. Not a happy moment!

Jack Haig was doing some comedy lines at rehearsals, and the director said "I've got enough comics in the show, you've got to play it straight!" Jack said, "But I'm a comic!" "I've got enough comics!" was the reply. Jack went down to his car, brought his golf clubs up to the stage, and started swinging them. The director said, "What are you doing?" Jack said "Practising shots for the golf, when I go to my holiday home out in Spain!" "We'll see about that!" shouted the director, who stormed off and phoned Head Office – who promptly told him to let Jack do comedy!

Our 13month old daughter, Naomi was very poorly during the season, due to numerous cats in the digs, with a cat tray right by the toilet. You'd be enthroned, not realising a window above you was open, and a cat would leap in through the open window. Not nice, but it did get things moving! Our bedroom window was in front of a 24 hour garage on a main road, so even that wasn't good.

We did several pantomimes in Dublin. *Sleeping Beauty* at the Gaiety Theatre in 1986 was a memorable one. Brendan Grace was one of the main stars, and one evening he asked us to go with him when he was performing at a big club to see his act. He picked us up, and when we got back, we had been burgled! The police said, it was probably gypsies and that they couldn't go into their camps. I never saw my nice leather jacket again, but they had stolen my tap shoes as well, so if you see a tap dancing gypsy in Ireland, ask him where he got his tap shoes from! (Maybe he's doing River Dance?) Luckily I had an old pair with me that I could use. We did a big Sunday Night TV *Live from the Gaiety*, which Brendan compered. He was very nice about us, and told the audience that he stood at the side of the stage during the pantomime watching us, and telling them that we were "real prcs"!

1989 was memorable because we were performing with Ronnie Corbett again. This was *Cinderella* at the Theatre Royal in Newcastle. Ronnie asked for us especially, and said: "You can get a lot more money playing Ugly Sisters, cos they can cut out the Broker's Men!" (which we had played in the pantomime with him before). We fell on our feet because Ronnie didn't want Number One or Two rooms, as they were straight across from the bar. So I ended up in Number One, and Jimmy in Number Two! It was lovely to be in rooms that huge stars had used. In fact, my room was used by the fabulous Stewart Granger, who followed us in! We enjoyed the show immensely. A lovely pantomime and great to be back with Ronnie, and it was good to perform in Dad's old stomping ground!

Ronnie asked for us once again at Bromley in 1991 for *Jack and the Beanstalk*. (This was the first of four great years at Bromley.) We were the Giant's Henchmen. We did lots of stuff with Ronnie, and lots of our own bits too. On the last night, Paul Henry, who had been a pal at Norwich, had a go at Jimmy for some reason, and I stood up for him. Paul said, "You two are all for Ronnie Corbett!" We obviously were, having worked with him such a lot! This marred our relationship somewhat, and we left on non-speaking terms – such a shame as we liked him very much. Ronnie was great, as always.

In 1992, while doing *Dick Whittington* in Edinburgh I got the flu. No, not a cold – full blown flu, so that – unknown for me – I had to miss a day's rehearsals as I just couldn't get up out of my sick bed. But we had a lovely flat fairly close to the theatre, and had a great season. Rachel and the children came up for Christmas and we had a lovely time, it even snowed on Christmas Day - magic!

Back as the Ugly Sisters at Bromley with Ronnie in 1993, for *Cinderella*. Janet Brown was the Fairy Godmother. She was a lovely lady. She "pranged" her car during rehearsals by running into the back of a police car - not a good thing to do! She ended up with a plaster cast on one arm in the show! She was an excellent pro, though, and carried on regardless. We loved being "sisters" again, and it was a great fun pantomime. We had incredible costumes, including one outfit which was all purple balloons, like a bunch of grapes – it was such a task making sure they didn't pop each performance, and I had to keep a supply in my dressing room. I had to have a personal dresser to make sure I hadn't deflated on my appearance!

The next year we did the same panto again, but moved to Cardiff, and this time they packed it with TV names – Carmen Silvera from *'Allo, 'Allo* as Fairy Godmother, and lovely Peter Byrne as Baron Hardup. Two guys from *That's Life*, Adrian Mills and Kevin Devine, were Prince and Dandini. Esther Rantzen came round with her husband, Desmond Wilcox, but it was like royalty! People standing in line, and we didn't even get to say hello! At the last night party, the lady manager of the New Theatre said "A big thank you" to all the staff, but no mention of Ronnie or the cast. Ronnie said in his speech "I think we had something to do with its success!" – which we all enjoyed hearing!

We should have been with Ronnie again for the 1995 production of *Aladdin* – back in Bromley (hooray!). We had lovely Gloria Hunniford topping the bill as Fairy Godmother. She was a smashing lady, who would come in for a chat at times whenever she was free. Bonnie Langford, another lovely talented lass, was Aladdin. Jimmy and I were the Chinese Policemen. Again, Ronnie had asked us to take part, but ended up not doing it himself! But we were all together again the next year, still in Bromley, in *Mother Goose*. Donald Hewlett couldn't remember his lines in the routine with Ronnie, and Ronnie said "How can I get laughs if the feed lines aren't there?" Donald had them written up on a big card in the Orchestra Pit! He was a lovely guy though. Unfortunately this was to be our last time working with Ronnie: he never did pantomime again, sadly. Magic Days.

We kept going of course, and there were plenty more memorable experiences. *Dick Whittington* in Preston in 1999 was a good one. The only trouble with Preston is the stairs, you go up two or three flights to get on to the stage and then back down again every time.

Rachel and I decided as a family, to go to Midnight Mass on Christmas Eve, and saw a church spire in the distance. We went to check on the times of the services, and when we got there it was a carpet warehouse! So on Christmas Eve we drove up to the parish church, but we were advised not to leave our car in the car park opposite as it was "dangerous". We drove past the church which was surrounded by police cars, and decided not to get out! Instead we found a service near our digs in a church hall, and the vicar arrived with his cassock tucked in to his trousers - he must have arrived on a bike!

In 2001 we made our first panto appearance with our brothers Paul and Barry topping the bill. This was *Aladdin* at Darlington Civic. It was a good family pantomime for the audience and us, and the business was very good indeed. It's the only time we didn't have our name out front at the theatre. It was just the lads, The Chuckle Brothers! We weren't on the hand bills either! Jimmy was Dame, and I played the Chinese Policeman. We enjoyed the pantomime and it was good to have all four of us together, and on the same dressing room floor, all in a row.

The family travelled up from Kent as a surprise for me on the train. Everyone seemed to know they were coming except me, and they had tickets booked and a hotel too! I heard a knock on the dressing room door and shouted, "Come In!" They came in laughing, as a lovely surprise. My son Damian who was 11 found my *Sunday Sport* under the chair, causing much hilarity. I still maintain I was just reading the sport!

Another memorable *Aladdin* was at Carlisle in 2006 – a short but lovely season. We stayed the whole time in a hotel, with breakfast laid on as part of the pantomime deal! It was a long cold walk to the theatre, but worth the trek from one side of Carlisle to the other (we drove several times). Jimmy's wife Val stayed for much of the season, and she and Rachel really enjoyed the town. We were top of the bill, and a very good director David McNeil. The dressing room was tiny, but we managed to change ok somehow. At the theatre we were given a meal at tea time every day, as part of the deal!

My lad Damian joined us for *Red Riding Hood* at Bolton in 2007. This was his first professional pantomime – he played the Wolf - and he shared our dressing room, which was lovely for me. (His Uncle Jimmy was great about it too. He's a great brother and partner.) We had a great time, and Ted Robbins in the title role was great to work with and a pleasure to know. He had a dressing room next door to us. He had a sleep every day between shows, and we could hear his loud snoring so always knew he was asleep!

Jack and the Beanstalk at the Bolton Macron Stadium in 2015 was another memorable one. This was a first for us, performing in a huge concert hall, with a stage with no scenery, only a white backcloth which had projected images to make up the scenery. There were no dressing rooms, but the dressing area could be viewed up on a huge balcony area, so the lights were kept off! The dressing rooms were made up of free standing screens and partitioned off, into tiny areas, with a small round table and one chair. No mirrors, or hanging area, so the costumes had to be hung over the top of the screens in the hope that the screens would not topple over! We made up in the toilets – you had to have a sense of humour. But nevertheless it was a most enjoyable pantomime!

Jimmy liked to have a rest between shows, so they found him a mattress to put into a quiet area. The rest of the cast were offered a room to rest in in the hotel, which was amazing, and which I took them up on. I regularly had a view of the empty football stadium, and could make tea and coffee and had a TV to watch between shows!

The pantomime was great fun, although the director could be quite forthright, which ended up with several of the actors throwing down costumes and walking out for a "cool down". Jimmy and I tried to pacify the situation, and the pantomime rehearsals continued the following day!

2016 was our last pantomime to date as a double act – *Aladdin* again, at Port Sunlight. Port Sunlight is a beautiful village, and we were very happy there for the season. Rachel and I stayed in a lovely hotel for Christmas for 6 days, about 9 miles away towards Chester. We found a beautiful little church in a place called Stoak for our Christmas day service, and they were so welcoming. I had flu for the last few weeks, but struggled through. Jimmy caught the same virus near the end of the pantomime. We like to share most things!

Some Panto Memories ...

STILL GOING STRONG

THE CHUCKLE BROTHERS

Jimmy:

Our two youngest brothers, Paul and Barry, used to watch us in shows when they were still at school. More recently they have been the stars of their own children's TV show *Chucklevision*. The lads took their chance with both hands when it came to them, and they ended up stars who packed theatres with family audiences wherever they went. Life is great for them, and they deserve their success.

Brian:

We had been offered *Opportunity Knocks*, but we decided against it as we had already performed at the London Palladium, and Frank Mansell at Butlins told us that he wouldn't be able to use us as comedians if we came second to a dog or something! Barry and Paul went on, and asked me to introduce them as 'The Harman Brothers', and they did very well. Hughie Green introduced me as "one of the famous Patton Brothers"! He also said "their mother, Jean Patton was in the business!" Dad loved the mention, but wasn't happy about becoming our mother, and one or two expletives followed the comment!

Jimmy:

What a lot of people don't know is that Brian and I appeared professionally alongside Paul and Barry at one time, all billed as The Chuckle Brothers. We did a few Sunday concerts for impresario Stanley Cher in the seventies, and Paul and Barry were on the same bill. We were the Patton Brothers; they were the Harman Brothers. Stanley said, "Why don't you merge together and make a foursome like the Marx Brothers?" So we worked out an act for the four of us, and called ourselves the Chuckle Brothers.

Brian:

We made our first TV appearance as the four Chuckle Brothers on *3-2-1* in 1980. We did a spot of knockabout comedy which went down really well, and can still be seen on YouTube. We then had to hand in a clue for the contestants to guess the cryptic message. It was great to see Ted Rogers again, of course, after doing several pantomimes with him. We followed that with *The Lennie and Jerry Show* with Lennie Bennett and Jerry Stevens, filmed at the Talk of the Town in London. Sitting in the first couple of rows were Argentinian football stars Ossie Ardilles and Ricardo Villa, and they were falling about when we were on stage! We also did *The Good Old Days* together, among others.

Jimmy:

Everyone loved the act but at the time we couldn't command the money needed for four people and a manager. We were an established act as the Patton Brothers, so Paul and Barry kept the name the Chuckle Brothers. Barry had thought of the name in the first place and it worked perfectly for them. The rest is history!

They got their big break by chance when they were touring in a children's show with ventriloquist Ward Allen and Roger the Dog. He was going to do his own TV show for the BBC and needed two people to dress as dogs in the programme. The lads said they'd do it and the 'Chucklehounds' were born. Their producer Martin Hughes liked the characters and gave them their own show. They were a big dog and a small dog, and did sketches and gags like Laurel and Hardy. It proved very successful, and after a couple of series Martin said, "The audiences don't know what you look like underneath those animal costumes." So in 1989 he devised *Chucklevision* for the 'real' Paul and Barry, and it became an institution on children's TV, running for 20 years and 21 series.

In 1989 the lads asked me to play a character in one of the episodes. It was a good part, as the manager of a hotel in Blackpool. They gave me a catchphrase too! Every time I gave them a job to do, I'd say: "Remember – no slacking!" Martin Hughes, the producer, liked my performance, and they used me in every series from then on.

Brian:

In the first one I did I played a vicar. I got sploshed - what a surprise! My next one was 'Oh Brother', where I pretended to be their long lost brother. I did a lot more episodes, but one of my favourites was 'The Incredible Shrinking Barry'. I also enjoyed the ones where the four of us appeared together. I played mainly different characters, shouting "Get out of it!" as my catchphrase.

Jimmy:

We both loved doing it, so we have a lot to thank Barry and Paul for, along with Martin and John Sayle, the show's writer. Through all that time the lads did a Chucklevision theatre tour each spring, and we shared a stage with them for fifteen great years. We all get on well together and always have, so it was wonderful to have all four brothers together again throughout that time.

Brian:

Harry Hill came to see *Chucklevision* at Croydon, and I was in the front of the theatre when he came in with a couple of youngsters. He was looking round and I said "Would you like to come and meet Barry and Paul?" He said "Love to", so I took them backstage. He said he loved *Chucklevision* and would like to be in one episode. He did a very funny episode with the lads called 'Mind your Manors'.

Editor's note:

Sadly, Barry Elliott, better known to millions as Barry Chuckle, passed away on August 5th, 2018, just as this book was going to press. In the days that followed Jimmy, Brian and Paul all paid tribute to a beloved brother and fellow performer, and it is fair to say that the nation took note with that special acuity it reserves for only the most warmly appreciated of personalities. It was a poignant but powerful reminder of how our lives are affected by the people who make us laugh.

Jimmy:

On the tours we would all travel together in a big motor home, playing cards and charades to pass the time. Touring the theatres with my brothers brought back some wonderful memories. When we played the Wyvern Theatre, Swindon, I remembered appearing at the Playhouse Theatre there in 1946, and the Empire Theatre in 1954. That was when the town was full of American servicemen. They loved our strip show, *Honky Tonk.* Most of these wonderful old variety theatres have gone now, but some still remain, like the Grand in Doncaster, the City Varieties in Leeds and the Collins Music Hall in Islington.

One of our proudest moments ever came in 1955, when we topped the bill at the Regent Theatre in our home town of Rotherham. There was a huge billboard over the railway bridge that must have been fifty yards long. There in massive letters was our names 'Jimmy and Brian Patton – Rotherham's Own Crazy Comedy Song and Dance Men.' It was a lovely week and all our friends came to see us. We got £20 for the week - £10 each! As we were top of the bill, we tipped the stage manager, the electrician, the musical director and the stage door keeper. As you can imagine, that didn't actually leave us with much! But it was a lovely time of life, and so rewarding to be doing a job we loved. We even had our own printed writing paper, printed envelopes and visiting cards! Now? Well, now an indoor market has replaced the old Regent. All the cinemas in Rotherham have gone, too. I spent so many happy hours at the Odeon, the Hippodrome, the Whitehall, the Cinema House, the Empire, the Tivoli and the Premier in the 1940s and 50s. Seven cinemas, all in close proximity and always full of happy people... now, all gone.

And how the business has changed since then! There were no live shows on Sundays in the 1940s, only films. No television either. Even in the 1950s the rules were still very stringent. All scripts had to be sent to the Lord Chamberlain for approval. When we opened on a Monday night in a new town with our show the Watch Committee would be in the audience to make sure that the script was adhered to and no blue material had crept in.

As for Sunday concerts, they were allowed by then but still with strict rules. We were playing a week at the Empire, Bristol, and on the Sunday they booked us into the Regal Cinema, Minehead. No dancing was permitted, so to get round it our boss Philip Hindin said, "Leave your tap shoes off and do your routine with pumps on." So there we were, tapping away, and not a sound was coming out!

Cross patter wasn't allowed on Sundays either. Single comics could tell gags, but not double acts. When we did Sunday concerts at the Winter Gardens, Morecambe, in 1959 we had to change the act and do comedy monologues and rhymes where we spoke separately to the audience and not to each other! It sounds unbelievable now, but that's how it was. Today, anything goes, but as for what they call 'alternative comedy', I think it's just ludicrous. Comedy is either funny or it isn't, and in my opinion these Channel 4 alternative comedians, with a few exceptions, are as funny as a kick in the cobblers. A true clown can make you laugh with just movement or a facial expression. Tommy Cooper would have you in hysterics before he did anything at all. What about that wonderful specialty act George Carl? He didn't utter a word: just fabulous slapstick comedy. And then there was Max Wall. In those black tights and long black wig he'd have you in fits of laughter with that brilliant eccentric dance routine after a hilarious bit at the piano. Sheer genius. No replacements for any of them.

Brian:

I had the pleasure of doing pantomime with Max at Swansea Empire in *Robinson Crusoe* when I was a young lad. I did a tap routine on stage with him during the show. He used to appear on the radio most Sundays, and travelled up to London to record it. We loved his little ditty that he used to sing at the end of his act on the radio. He played a nice guitar as well in the pantomime.

It's been interesting to see how things have changed over the years. In 1967 we did a great season with the Black and White Minstrels at the Coventry Theatre. Jimmy and I were doing a spot in the show and firstly we went on as Batman and Robin, and ended up performing a tap routine. We decided to not wear the full Batman and Robin outfits but to put the masks on so that we were in suits for the act, which seemed to work better. We had a lovely picture taken with the girl dancers as Batman and Robin. George Mitchell's future wife, Dorothy, was also in the show. Today the Minstrels are very badly thought of, for no reason at all really. The audiences loved them right up until the middle 1980s. The cheers in the finale were unbelievable, the best we've ever heard for a show.

So here we are, in 2017! It'll be nice to put my feet up for this Christmas at last, and at 83, why not? I think I deserve it! It'll be nice to go up to

Whitley Bay and see our son Damian and his double act partner Tom Rolfe (they call their act 'Double Trouble') as Ugly Sisters in *Cinderella*, and for our daughter to be able to come home for Christmas. Naomi is a lovely oboist and now works at a music publishers close to the London Palladium. Damian is married to a talented actress, Jade, and they live down in Somerset. Hey, we could even dust off the non-travelling Christmas tree at last!

Jimmy:

Our 2016 pantomime, playing the Chinese Policemen in *Aladdin* was our 58th together. It's a long way from the day I set off from Rotherham on September 23rd, 1946, to start my stage career with Britain's Dead End Kids. Then in 1954 Brian and I became The Patton Brothers and we've had a wonderful career full of marvellous memories and met some great friends and colleagues along the way. We haven't finished yet as we have already been offered panto together next year if we want it.

We've had a wonderful life and met some wonderful people, and through our children the story goes on! Brian mentioned his children following in his footsteps in the business. It's the same with me: my daughter Debbie is a great dancer and choreographer and did panto and summer-seasons with Cannon and Ball, Joe Longthorne and Keith Harris. My son Lee has been the entertainments' manager at lots of holiday camps. Debbie now has her own dancing school, the Debonair Dance Academy in the West Midlands, whilst Lee is general manager of a holiday park in Ayr.

I've mentioned my first wife Val throughout the book. We were together for 47 great years, until she died from cancer of the pancreas in 2010. I was with her at her bedside holding her hand when she passed away, and it felt like my life was over too.

But then I met Amy in 2014, and three years later we were happily married and life is wonderful again. Amy and I have so much in common as she loves show business, and has always loved variety and films from way back to the golden years of Hollywood. Our wedding day in Southport was just lovely. She travelled over by train and we met at Sheffield Station and it was just like *Brief Encounter*!

Brian and I have certainly seen some changes in show business since I started but we still love it just as much. I wouldn't change a thing of our 63 years together. He's a wonderful brother and a great straight man and a superb tap dancer. Thank you, Brian, for a brilliant life together.

Love you, kid.

Lightning Source UK Ltd.
Milton Keynes UK
UKHW021817040819
347383UK00016B/442/P